Classic
American Automobiles

1914 *Locomobile*

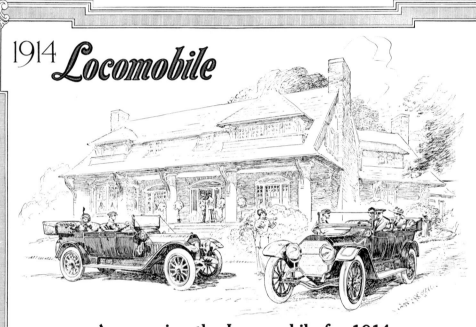

Announcing the Locomobile for 1914

Right Drive Models and Left Drive Models with Gear Lever operated by the Right Hand

ESTABLISHED as the easiest riding and best built car, with individual beauty of line and finish, the Locomobile is presented for 1914 in right drive and left drive models. On all cars control of the change gear lever is by the Right Hand, the safest and most natural arrangement.

Compare the Locomobile with other cars for comfort, beauty, mechanical excellence and firmness at high speeds. In a competitive test over the same course, we believe the Locomobile will outpoint any other in all features contributing to the greatest satisfaction of the owner.

A new, distinctive body type for 1914 is the six passenger Torpedo on the Big Six chassis; an original presentation. Closed cars include the Locomobile Berline and Berline Landaulet, models of distinctive atmosphere and elegance, and a new type of Limousine and Limousine Landaulet with sloping roof lines.

New Features for 1914

New Carbureter — built to meet demand of owners of high grade cars for maximum fuel efficiency and economy; makes the Locomobile an unusually economical high grade six.

New Tire Brackets — at rear, hold tires in place by metal band. Locking device prevents theft of tires.

Crank Case Oil Drain — oil in engine base lowered without getting under car.

Starting Crank Removed — and placed in tool kit — improves beauty of car.

Nickel Trimmings — rich in appearance, easy to keep clean.

Easiest Riding — rear springs free to move at both ends absorb all road shocks; Ten-Inch

Upholstery; seat cushions fit under upholstery on back; perfect balance of weight.

New Wrinkle-Proof Top — special form of bow construction supporting top in 6 points makes it wrinkle-proof when raised.

New Fenders — concealed rivets and rounded surfaces; harmonize with clean lines of car.

New Storage Compartment — at back of front seat, for side curtains, canes and umbrellas. Reached without disturbing occupants.

Air Adjustment — on steering post, provides regulation of mixture from seat. Gives smoothest running motor under all driving conditions.

New Lamps — of octagonal design, harmonizing with general decorative scheme of car.

Advanced Equipment — 70-mile speedometer, electric horn, Locomobile air compressor for inflating tires, rain vision wind shield, robe rail, foot rest, quick detachable tires and demountable rims.

Electric Motor Starter — an unfailing success since it was first adopted, continued as regular equipment on all Locomobiles for 1914.

New Priming Device — operated from dash, injecting gasolene in intake manifold. Ensures easy starting in all weather.

Electric Lighting — brightest lights and a system that never gives trouble.

SIX CYLINDER MODELS

"38" Left Drive Models and Right Drive Models   **"48" Left Drive Models and Right Drive Models**

Special folder now ready giving additional information regarding Locomobile cars for 1914, together with complete specifications of all models. Further printed matter showing cars in colors and giving more complete details mailed on request.

THE LOCOMOBILE COMPANY OF AMERICA, BRIDGEPORT, CONN.
Motor Cars and Motor Trucks

BRANCHES: NEW YORK   CHICAGO   PHILADELPHIA   BOSTON   WASHINGTON   BALTIMORE   SAN FRANCISCO
          ST. LOUIS   ATLANTA   PITTSBURGH   MINNEAPOLIS   BRIDGEPORT   LOS ANGELES   OAKLAND

Galahad Books • New York City

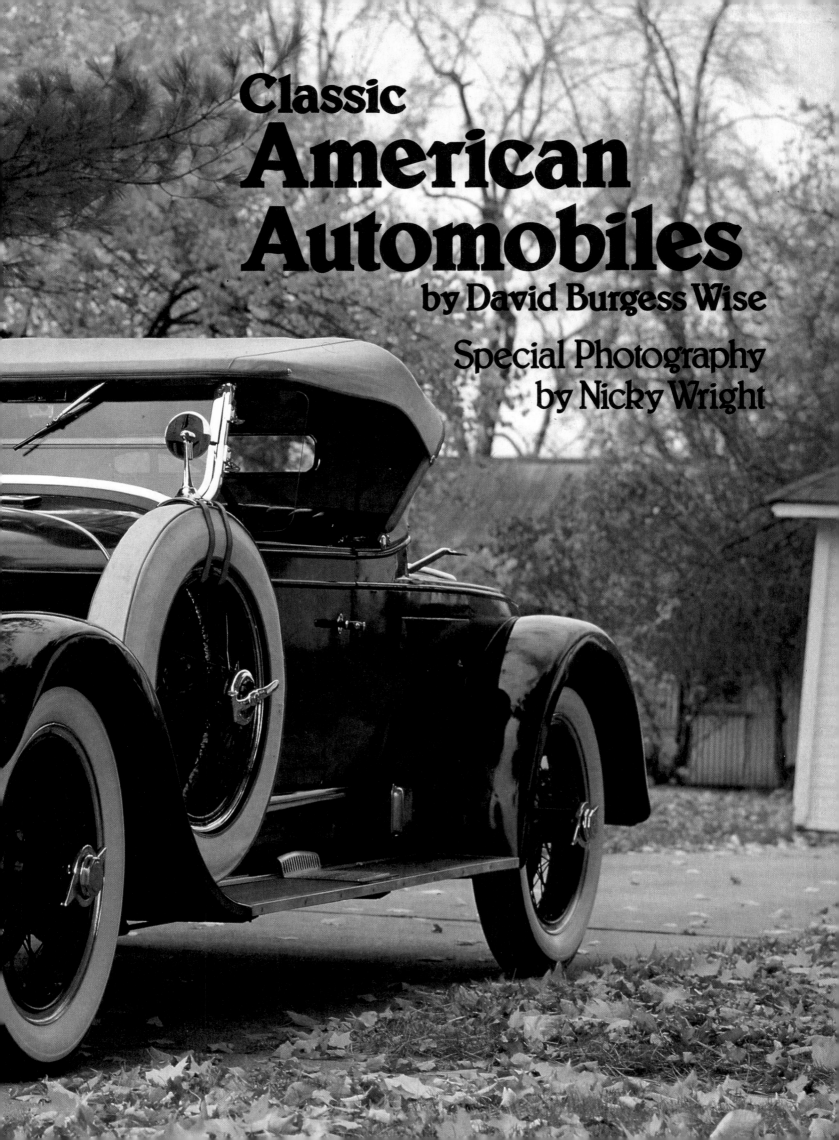

Classic
American
Automobiles

by David Burgess Wise

Special Photography
by Nicky Wright

Acknowledgments
We would like to thank Nicky Wright who supplied most of the
photographs for this book and also the following museums and
individuals for their especial help and cooperation: The
Auburn-Cord-Duesenberg Museum, Auburn, Ind.; Harrah's
Automobile Collection, Reno, Nevada; The Briggs
Cunningham Museum, Costa Mesa, Ca.; Otis Chandler;
Ernie Kay; Jimmy Duffy III; Hillcrest Motors, Beverly Hills,
Ca.; A. F. Mittermiar; Frank Kleptz; Paris Zarribian; Paul
Dexler; Mike Palumbo; Gary Goers; Harold and Richard
Carpenter; Jack Randinelli; Craig Sanderson; Dan Berger;
Skip Marketti; Hadzera Wright and Val Danneskold.

Designed and produced by
Albany Books
36 Park Street London W1Y 4DE

First published 1980
Reprinted in 1981

Published in the United States of
America by Galahad Books
95 Madison Avenue New York
New York 10016

House Editor: Miranda Harvey
Art Direction: Elizabeth Cooke
Design: Junita Grout

ISBN 0 88365 454 7
Library of Crongress Catalog Card Number: 80 66943

Text photoset in 12/14 pt Plantin 110
by SX Composing Limited, Rayleigh, Essex

Printed and bound in Spain by Printer Industria Gráfica, S.A.
D.L.B. 24305-1981

FRONT ENDPAPER: Engine detail from the 1908 Albany Model G
*(D. Welch, Auburn-Cord-Duesenberg Museum. Photo: Nicky
Wright)*

BACK ENDPAPER: Engine detail from the 1931 Model J
Duesenberg *(Auburn-Cord-Duesenberg Museum. Photo: Nicky
Wright)*

PAGE 5: Advertisement for the Locomobile of 1914
(Contemporary illus. The Saturday Evening Post)

PAGES 6 AND 7: The Model A Duesenberg *(Homer Fitterling,
Auburn-Cord-Duesenberg Museum. Photo: Nicky Wright)*

PAGE 9: The 1929 Peerless Six-81 3.7-litre sedan was powered
by a Continental Six. A V8 was also available that year *(Keith
Marvin)*

Contents

1 Prelude to the

Twenties

The automobile came late to the United States. Only a handful of pioneers built cars before 1900 and production was minimal. Only 8000 cars were registered in the USA in 1900 and half of those were actually built in that year as output began to gain momentum at last. The reason for this late start is not hard to find for, geographically, America was an inimical environment for this new means of locomotion.

America was a newly settled continent and consequently had no national road system like that which had grown in Europe since the days of the Romans. Roads scarcely existed outside the cities. All long-distance travel had become the monopoly of the railroad since 10 May 1869 when the transcontinental railway, laid from the west by the Central Pacific Railroad and from the east by the Union Pacific, was completed by the 'linking of the rails' at Promontory Point, Utah (the two locomotives 'Jupiter' and 'No. 119' had met head-to-head, 'facing on the single track, half a world behind each back'). There was thus little incentive to establish long-distance roads; the vast distances and the slow speed of horse-drawn vehicles were hardly conducive to inter-city travel.

At the turn of the century America was still largely rural. Half of the inhabitants of the United States lived either on farms, of which there were some six million nationwide, or in towns of under 2500 inhabitants. So America's first automobiles were novelties – impracticable toys for the wealthy. In 1900, the year in which the Automobile Club of America held its first 'Automobile Exposition' in New York, the newly founded magazine *Automobile Topics* recorded:

The automobile has been extensively taken up by society, and during the past season in Newport and Lenox it played a most important part in social life. Women like Mrs Stuyvesant Fish, Mrs Herman Oelrichs, Mrs Wm. K. Vanderbilt Jr., and others who are noted for their daring in taking up sports which have the merit of unconventionality, will not be satisfied until they have driven their motor carriages through the city streets.

PAGES 10 AND 11: 1908 Zimmerman Model B Runabout, typical of the high-wheeled cars designed for rural American roads (*Auburn-Cord-Duesenberg Museum. Photo: Nicky Wright*)

RIGHT: Designed for society ladies, the electric car enjoyed a fashionable following in America in the early 1900s (*Contemporary illus.*)

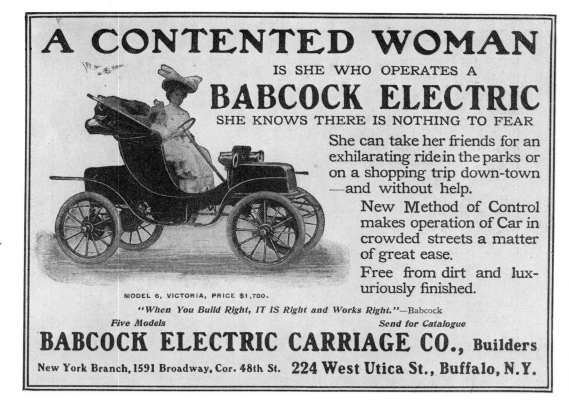

ABOVE: Alexander Winton (left) at the wheel of his *Bullet* racer built for the 1903 Gordon Bennett Cup Race in Ireland (DBW)

Early motorists had little opportunity for driving their cars anywhere except on urban roads. Despite the fact that there were probably as many bicycles as horses in the USA in the late 1890s – perhaps ten million of them – touring by road was almost impossible. Certainly towns and hamlets were linked by tracks but these had simply been carved by the wheels of carts, carriages and Conestoga waggons and became impassable morasses in winter rain. The powerful cycling lobby was already calling for the construction of hard-surfaced roads but to little avail. The first motorists who cautiously ventured on to rural roads were likely to find their vehicles mired down to the axles in glutinous mud from which they might have to be towed by a team of horse or oxen. Just how bad the situation had become is shown by the census held by the newly revived United States Office of Road Inquiry, published in 1904. It showed that, of the two million miles of roads in the USA, all but 150,000 miles were 'unimproved', a euphemism for dirt-tracks. Of the 'improved' highways, most had merely a thin sprinkling of gravel and only 250 miles (apart from city streets) were actually paved.

Nevertheless there were some foolhardy souls intent on demonstrating the touring capabilities of the automobile. Alexander Winton, a Scottish engineer who had become one of America's leading automobile manufacturers, set off from San Francisco in May 1901 determined to make the first ever crossing of the United States by car. 'For the first few miles the going was excellent,' a contemporary report noted, 'but the intrepid motorists soon realised the terrible nature of their journey, and finally the quicksands of Nevada proved the intrepid voyagers' Waterloo. The machine sank into the soft soil until the wheels could barely be seen, and after vain efforts to extricate the car, the plucky riders lugubriously gave up their transcontinental attempt.'

It was two years before another trans-America automobile trip was attempted. The chosen vehicle was again a Winton, driven by Dr H. Nelson Jackson and Sewall K. Crocker. This time they went prepared for the worst; their equipment, strapped in an ungainly, 3-ft high bundle to the

tailboard of their 20hp car included, 'in addition to the general personal perquisites, shovels for digging out the car at difficult points, axes for removing fallen trees, hammers, rope and tackle for hoisting the car over parts otherwise impossible to negotiate, supplies for the machine . . .' Benefiting from Winton's experiences, Jackson and Crocker took a circuitous route to attempt to bypass the worst road conditions but found that their way consisted of: 'scarcely visible horse tracks, which gave more trouble than if the motorists had set off across untrodden ground. To cross the mountain torrents it was imperative to make the car temporarily amphibious, since there were no bridges . . . No traces of civilisation were met with and the party suffered terrible privations'. On one occasion they ran out of petrol and Crocker had to walk almost thirty miles to find more fuel. On another day, stuck fast in desert quicksand for thirty-six hours, they ran out of food and were only saved from starvation by discovering the camp of an itinerant sheep-herder.

The 'bad lands' of Wyoming posed particular difficulties. When crossing Elk Mountain they tried to follow the old horse-waggon trail and found that 'the ruts were so deep that the axles of the car struck the crown of the trail,

leaving the wheels spinning idly in the air'. After that, the rest of the journey proved relatively easy and the Winton eventually rolled into New York sixty-five days after leaving San Francisco.

Already the second transcontinental motor journey was under way with Tom Fetch driving a 12hp Packard which took sixteen days for the crossing. Just sixteen days after Tom Fetch's trip, the third successful crossing of the continent began. This journey, which was to take seventy-four days, was – in many ways – the most significant until then. While the Winton and the Packard were, by American standards, relatively highly-priced machines, the vehicle undertaking this trip was an example of America's first popular, mass-produced petrol car. This was a 5hp 'Curved Dash' Oldsmobile, which was being produced at the rate of 4000 to 5000 annually, thanks to flow-production methods which brought in materials and components, as they were needed, to the assembly crews of men, each of whom had a specific task.

The Oldsmobile, although it was crude and basic in many ways, exemplified the type of car that was to appeal to rural America in the early part of the twentieth century. It had excellent ground clearance and low-speed

ABOVE: America's first mass-produced petrol car, the 'Curved-Dash' Oldsmobile, had a single-cylinder 5hp engine under the seat (*Photo: Nicky Wright*)

torque; high speed and elaborate finish were unnecessary. Furthermore, because America lacked a reserve of skilled engineers and craftsmen such as those who existed in Europe, the only way that cars could be built cheaply was to design them so that the costly skills could be employed in designing and making machines to reproduce the car components in large numbers. These components could then be assembled by unskilled labour with each man being given an individual task to perform. It was a technique that had been well proven in the field of arms manufacture – and it was in that field that one of the outstanding automotive engineers of the early days, Henry Leland (founding father of both Cadillac and Lincoln), had received his training and earned his soubriquet of 'the Master of Precision'.

Oldsmobile was also significant in being the first major manufacturer to start building cars in Detroit. This city had become a focus of motor activity as early as 1896 when both Charles Brady King and Henry Ford had built prototype horseless carriages. The Olds Motor Works was set up in 1899 with backing from the Detroit copper king Samuel L. Smith and began – unsuccessfully – to market costly $1250 cars. Then the Olds factory, on East Jefferson Street in Detroit, burned down after a gas explosion. Only the prototype 'Curved Dash' runabout was saved – a fortuitous survival for it was this machine that was to make Oldsmobile famous. Moreover Henry Leland's company, Leland and Faulconer, was called in to supply the engines and the Dodge brothers' machine shop was given the contract to supply transmissions thus bringing together into the industry the two firms that were to make a major contribution to motor history. Though Oldsmobile production was soon shifted to Lansing, Michigan, attracted by a fifty-two acre site donated by the Lansing Businessmen's Association, the seed had been sown for Detroit to become the centre of car manufacture.

Another early stalwart of the Detroit motor industry was Henry B. Joy, wealthy son of a railroad tycoon, who was to 'put the badge of social

prestige upon automobile manufacturing'. Joy, unable to find a car in Detroit that would suit him (Henry Ford is reputed to have refused to sell Joy one of his early productions because it was still experimental) went to New York with his brother-in-law, Truman H. Newberry. Here he was impressed with the easy starting of a car built in Warren, Ohio, by an electrical engineer named James Ward Packard (the town of Warren, incidentally, had been named after James's father, Warren Packard) who had gone into motor manufacturing because he felt he could build a better car than the Winton he had just acquired, which had chiefly distinguished itself by breaking down with alarming regularity. Joy bought the Packard car and was so impressed with it that he bought the production rights to it as well. He persuaded his wealthy Detroit friends to back the venture and set up a plant in Detroit to build 'the kind of car the aristocrats would like to drive'.

Joy knew that the kind of car 'the aristocrats' wanted was a European one for, in terms of styling and engineering, the Europeans were unbeatable. The original Packard had merely been a superior form of the typical American 'gas buggy', distinguished principally by its pioneering use of automatic spark advance, the invention of James Ward Packard. Joy wanted to be able to build a car of the type that was being shipped from Europe for wealthy Americans, but at a price free from all the loadings of import duty and freight costs that such vehicles carried. He therefore hired a French engineer, Charles Schmidt, to develop a new four-cylinder model. James Packard himself had resolutely set his face against anything but single-cylinder cars, believing that extra cylinders only multiplied the chances of mechanical problems.

Schmidt's first four, the Model K, appeared in 1904. This was followed a year later by Model L, significant in that it was the first Packard to bear the shouldered 'yoke-shaped' radiator and the indented hexagons in the hub cap which were to be the distinguishing sign of all the classic Packards.

Model K, however, was used as the basis of the famous 'Gray Wolf' racer that brought so much publicity to the marque at that period, driven by its designer. 'Gray Wolf', a pointed-nose bolide capable of over 90mph, was theoretically available as a catalogue model, provided that the prospective customer could produce the necessary $10,000.

Henry Joy later recalled that in the first year under his control, Packard built 200 cars and lost $200,000 but, despite that setback, he called for production to be doubled to 400 the next season. He had pledged his wealthy friends who held shares in the company that, so long as he was prepared to back Packard financially, they would match his stake dollar for dollar. 'And soon the Packard began to demonstrate that a man did not have to be reared with grease stains around his fingernails and callouses on his palms to be a successful automobile manufacturer.'

France was not the only source of design talent for erstwhile manufacturers of luxury cars. When cycle makers George N. Pierce, of Buffalo, New York (who had started in business in 1865 as makers of cages for pet birds and squirrels) decided to enter the infant motor industry, they appointed an Englishman to design their first production vehicle. David Fergusson, from Bradford in Yorkshire, had arrived in the States under somewhat dubious circumstances, accompanying the notorious 'motor charlatan' Edward Joel Pennington.

Pennington, who had found England too hot to hold him and his appalling designs (he had made a considerable sum selling his specious patents but had failed to deliver cars against cash orders received), had decided to visit his native America to promote his latest invention, a 'war-torpedo land-machine', leaving behind a bankruptcy order which stated that 'he owed £16,000, had no means and was living at the rate of £30 a week'. In New York, Pennington was singularly unsuccessful in interesting the American Government in his 'immense travelling masked battery with a crew of eight or ten on board and half a dozen guns' and his associates began to drift away.

David Fergusson found work with the E. C. Stearns Company of Syracuse, New York, and began work on a petrol car. Finding that his employers were more interested in steam power, he moved to Pierce where his first design was a 2¾hp voiturette on the lines of the French De Dion, introduced in 1901. Fergusson progressed through various single- and twin-cylinder models until, in 1904, he launched his classic Great Arrow four-cylinder 24/28hp. This elegant machine, which had a 3770cc engine, was very much in the Mercedes idiom, and had a pressed-steel chassis (the earliest Pierces had used tubular frames). It was joined the next year by similar models of 30hp and 40hp. Fortuitously, that was the year of the first Glidden Tour and one of the new 30hp models was to win this gruelling, prestigious event that was to do so much to establish the credentials of the American motor industry. At that period the industry was being riven by an attempt by the agents of George Baldwin Selden to establish a patents monopoly on the concept of the motor car under the auspices of the ALAM (Association of Licensed Automobile Manufacturers).

The Glidden Tour was the brainchild of Charles Jasper Glidden, who had made a fortune in the telephone industry and had retired in his early forties to indulge his ambition of driving a motor car round the world, planning to cover 50,000 miles between 1901 and 1911 in his 24hp Napier, built in London. By 1904 he had circled the globe twice and had driven across the Arctic Circle 1000 miles further north than any car had ever

BELOW: Headlamp from the 22hp Metz (*Harrah's, Reno, Nevada. Photo: Nicky Wright*)

been. He decided to promote an endurance run that would put the products of the infant American automobile industry to a searching practical test. In 1904 he gave his name to a loosely organised run of 1964 miles from New York to St Louis, with no rules and no prizes, and was so encouraged when sixty-six out of seventy-seven starters survived the distance that he decided to offer an ornate trophy for a reliability event designed to 'stimulate American automobile development'.

Over the next few years manufacturers were to spend, if not a king's, at least a captain of industry's ransom, in attempting to win this arduous, long-distance event which, in the period up to 1910, favoured the higher-powered, costlier cars. During that time the Glidden Trophy was virtually a Pierce prerogative. The marque used the Glidden as a forcing ground for development. In 1906 an experimental six-cylinder took part, to be translated into production terms the following year. (From 1910 the marque, which had by now bowed to the inevitable and had hyphenated itself as 'Pierce-Arrow', offered nothing but six-cylinder cars). Pierce won the Glidden in 1905, 1906, 1907 and 1909 (in 1908 the Glidden trophy was not awarded as three teams out of ten entered gained perfect scores, although the Pierce-Arrow won the subsidiary Hower Trophy after a tie-breaker run between the first five cars). Thereafter the rules were recast to give the lesser models a chance, and the Glidden was finally abandoned after a team of friction-drive Metz (a utilitarian machine originally sold piece by piece by instalment mail-order) had carried off the Trophy in the 1913 run. The prototype six which had competed in 1906 was the progenitor of one of the most prestigious pachyderms in the early history of the American motor industry, the Pierce-Arrow 66hp, of which 1638 were built over a period of ten years. Along with the 1916 aeroengined Fageol, the 66 was America's largest ever production model. From 1912 its massive power unit, with

BELOW LEFT: A 22hp Metz similar to this car won the 1913 Glidden Trophy, upsetting makers of luxury cars (*Harrah's, Reno, Nevada. Photo: Nicky Wright*)

BELOW RIGHT: Pierce-Arrow 48hp roadster of 1915 vintage. Its six-cylinder engine displaces 7.4 litres (*Briggs Cunningham Automotive Museum. Photo: Nicky Wright*)

each cylinder cast separately, had a displacement of 13,514cc and this perfectly proportioned giant rode on a 12ft 3½in wheelbase.

The Glidden Tour, by promoting 'greater endurance and reliability over bad roads', helped to develop a particularly robust type of quality car in America. Yet these vehicles were rarely seen outside their homeland. One reason why American cars were treated with some suspicion in Europe was because, during the bicycle boom of the 1890s, American manufacturers had flooded the European market with cheap, badly finished cycles that rapidly fell to pieces. The first American cars therefore inherited an evil — and not always deserved — reputation.

American cars sold in Europe because of their cheapness. Their other virtues went largely unrecorded although, in 1908, the enterprising Cadillac agent Fred S. Bennett gave a convincing demonstration of the rigorous interchangeability of the Cadillac's components by dismantling three cars, jumbling the parts in a shed in the newly opened Brooklands racetrack (and adding components of a fourth car for good measure) and then assembling three completely operable cars from the random heaps — with none of the hand fitting, filing and scraping then considered necessary by even the most prolific European manufacturers. For this feat, which caused something of a stir in the Americanophobe motor papers, Cadillac won the prestigious Dewar Trophy.

The Cadillac of 1908 was still a low-priced motor car, and no amount of kudos gained from a demonstration of its engineering excellence could give it social standing. An example of this problem is shown by a Ford model. Incidentally, the first Ford and Cadillac production models were remarkably similar for both were the work of Henry Ford, who had resigned from the Henry Ford Company — subsequently renamed Cadillac — to found the Ford Motor Company in 1903. The Ford company, having been associated with gas buggies from its inception, brought out a luxury six-cylinder, 40hp, Model K, in 1906 at the behest of Henry Ford's backers who felt that bigger profits reposed in the luxury car market. It sold moderately well in the States, despite a somewhat fragile two-speed epicyclic transmission, but attempts to market it in Europe were a total failure. Only two were sold,

and those by more than usually forceful methods: anyone who paused to look in the London showrooms of the importers – and who appeared reasonably well-heeled – was immediately dragged inside by the ever-watchful salesmen.

Part of the trouble was because the higher-priced American cars were rather utilitarian in appearance. Some years ago I rode in a 1908 Thomas-Flyer, one of the finest American cars of its day, and mechanically identical to the Thomas which won that year's 25,000-mile New York–Paris Race. A rare, fast, and finely proportioned machine, the Thomas-Flyer was definitely lacking in the detail refinements and rich finish that one would have expected from a European car of similar prestige. An English or French car, for instance, might have been six months at the coachbuilders having a luxuriously bespoke body fitted, painted and varnished. Such was the pace of progress in the first decade of this century that it might have become obsolescent before its owner took the completed vehicle for its first drive. The Thomas-Flyer's touring coachwork looked, by comparison, distinctly 'off-the-peg' and more than a little homely.

American buyers who were looking for fine coachwork therefore bought European cars and had them shipped in through the East Coast ports despite a swingeing import duty. Possibly the careless payment of this unnecessary impost (implying limitless wealth) may have appealed to the

ABOVE: Henry Ford is at the wheel of this big 1906 Ford Model K 40/50hp six-cylinder, pictured in New York City (DBW)

super rich who wished to flaunt their fortunes. Larz Anderson, for example, imported a gigantic French CGV limousine of around 13.5 litres, whose engine had to be fitted with a geared-down starting handle so that the chauffeur could actually turn it over. This mighty power unit was necessary for the behemoth whose huge limousine bodywork concealed a capacious water tank which supplied a built-in lavatory . . .! Some companies attempted to offer the snobbish cachet of an imported car in combination with an 'all-American' price. Such a firm was Viqueot of Long Island City who bought chassis from a manufacturer in Puteaux, near Paris, imported them into America and fitted them with American bodywork. The viability of that exercise can be gauged by the fact that the company only lasted a year.

Other manufacturers bought ready-made European designs. The American Locomotive Company, one of America's best-known manufacturers of railway engines, built cars under licence from a fellow locomotive maker, the French Berliet company of Lyon, from 1905. Berliet (still in business as makers of trucks) were then building cars of superlative quality closely patterned on the Mercedes. Known from 1905 to 1908 as 'American Berliet' and from 1908 to the end of production in 1913 as 'Alco', these cars were built in a factory in Providence, Rhode Island. Alco, who twice won the Vanderbilt Cup – America's principal motor race – described their products in one advertisement as 'breaking away from the old, the commonplace, the stereotyped – and in their stead the original, the beautiful . . . the ultra in the Alco'.

At that time, oddly enough, the American Locomotive Company was having some problems with its railway activities and had called in a young 'railroad shopman, roundhouse foreman, superintendent of motive power and so forth' called Walter P. Chrysler. Yet Chrysler, who had borrowed $4300 a short while before to buy a Locomobile car and had visions of going into car manufacture on his own account, never made the move from the American Locomotive works at Pittsburgh, Pa., to the Alco factory. Instead he took a salary cut from $12,000 to $6000 annually to become superintendent of the Buick car works at Flint, Michigan.

Smith & Mabley, whose showrooms at 513–519 Seventh Avenue, New York, were the Mecca for those who wished to buy a top quality European car in the early years of this century, took a slightly different course from Alco. They were agents for Mercedes, Panhard and Renault, and for a mere $12,750 they offered the wealthy motorist a 28/32hp Mercedes with 'Vedrine King of the Belgians' coachwork, a dashing machine with ploughshare front wings, tulip-backed seats, wicker luncheon baskets and umbrella holder, and a canopy supported on iron stanchions. But 40 per cent of its price represented import duty and, reckoned Smith & Mabley, they could match Mercedes quality in a home-built product at half the cost. So in 1904 they added the 18hp S & M Simplex to their catalogue, a slightly less refined copy of the Mercedes. It had, for instance, a simple angle-iron chassis instead of the pressed-steel frame of the Mercedes and sold, with similar body and equipment to the German car, at only $6750.

Smith & Mabley had powerful patronage. When, later in the year, they uprated the touring Simplex to 30hp, Smith & Mabley also listed a 14·7 litre 'special 75hp' racing model, one of which was supplied to young Frank Croker. His father was the notorious 'Boss' Croker, who headed New York's corrupt Tammany Hall political organisation. Young Frank fancied himself as a racing driver and entered for the eliminating trials for the 1904

Vanderbilt Cup Race. The Special 75 was considerably over the weight limit for the event and consequently its chassis had to be drilled liberally to remove surplus metal. During the race it gradually folded in the middle and finished with its gearbox dragging a furrow in the road. Smith & Mabley fitted a new chassis and Frank took it down to Ormonde Beach to compete in the January 1905 speed trials where he wrote off the car in spectacular fashion, rolling it into the sea and killing himself. The French magazine *La Vie Au Grand Air*, always fond of publishing photos of smashed racing cars, illustrated the wreckage – a lacework of drilled and twisted steel lying on the foreshore with the surf washing over it.

This marked the end of Smith & Mabley's sporting ambitions and thereafter they listed only the 30hp alongside the imports. Then, in 1907, a recession in the motor business drove them out of business. Feeling that the marque deserved to be saved, Herman Broesel bought the remains and engaged the designer Edward Franquist to create a new, even more luxurious Simplex. Franquist once again followed the Mercedes path but this time there was no talk of substituting cheap materials. 'Finest gun iron' was used for casting cylinders and pistons, and Krupp's chrome nickel steel was employed for the chassis frame. The new Simplex company made virtually everything in their own works save for the tyres, electrical equipment and, of course, coachwork, which was bespoken from the finest bodybuilders of the day. Moreover, the reincarnated Simplex frequently – and successfully – appeared in competition, chiefly in endurance events which proved its durability, like the 24-hour race on the one-mile Brighton Beach dirt-track at the Coney Island pleasure grounds which George Robertson won two years in succession. The first year (1908) he covered 1177 miles at an average of 49mph, including a delay caused when he knocked down a track policeman. In 1909 he circled the track 1091 times, finishing 50 miles ahead of the next car.

ABOVE: The 1907 Thomas-Flyer 60hp which won the 25,000 mile New York-Paris Motor Race of 1908 (DBW)

23

RIGHT: Progenitor of a famous line – the first production Franklin air-cooled car was the transverse-four 12hp of 1904–05 (DBW)

WEDDING UNDER BIG TREE STANLEY PARK. VANCOUVER. B.C.

BELOW: Another fine American make was the Chadwick, whose 1906 racing cars were the first to use superchargers (*Keith Marvin*)

The Chadwick

1907

The marque's racing success prompted Franquist to bring out two new models: a 7·8-litre shaft-drive touring car which appeared in 1911 and the huge 10-litre 75hp sporting chassis, announced in 1912. This stark machine was almost certainly the last new chain-drive chassis to be introduced in America and, apart from cyclecars, the last chain-drive car in production, surviving until 1914. By that time ownership of Simplex had passed from Broesel to a triumvirate called Goodrich, Lockhardt and Smith. They also acquired the Crane Motor Company, which had been building $8000 cars at Bayonne, New Jersey, since 1912, and they appointed Henry M. Crane as designer in place of Franquist.

Crane brought out a magnificent 46hp six-cylinder, known variously as the Crane-Simplex or Simplex, Crane Model No. 5. It cost $10,000 in chassis form, and custom coachwork by leading builders like Brewster could make a substantial addition. It did not have, however, the sporting cachet of the old Simplex and was produced only until 1917. Even then production had so far outstripped sales that unsold chassis were still being fitted with new coachwork and presented as new cars as late as 1921.

There were other 'home-grown' luxury cars in the early days. In 1902 Andrew L. Riker, previously known as a designer of spindly electric carriages, created an excellent four-cylinder petrol car for Locomobile, who were trying to move away from the manufacture of frail steam buggies with an unenviable reputation for committing suttee at the slightest provocation. Riker's car, with pressed steel chassis, proved so attractive that by 1903 Locomobile were out of steam production altogether. They had become makers of expensive luxury cars and in 1904 offered two models on Mercedes lines, the 'Type C' 9/12hp twin-cylinder and the 16/22hp 'Type D' which, at over $5000 including limousine coachwork, was one of America's most expensive cars. Throughout the first decade of the twentieth century, Locomobiles became more powerful and more expensive. In 1909,

BELOW: The 46hp Crane Simplex was a total change of image for a company that had made its name building stark sports cars (*Keith Marvin*)

When the Milanese began the cathedral in 1386, no one asked "How much for the money?" The cathedral was four hundred years building; but the Vision was achieved.

That willingness to take infinite pains is what makes the blown glass of Venice, silk rugs of Persia, the shawls of India, the embroidered screens of Japan.

It is what makes the Crane Model Simplex.

"Neither snow, nor rain, nor heat, nor gloom of night stays these couriers from the swift completion of their appointed rounds." —Herodotus

ABOVE: 1913 Simplex 75hp chain-drive roadster with a 10-litre four-cylinder power unit (*Briggs Cunningham Automotive Museum. Photo: Nicky Wright*)

RIGHT: The 1913 Simplex 75hp chain-drive roadster, showing the side of the hood and part of the interior at the front (*Briggs Cunningham Automotive Museum. Photo: Nicky Wright*)

shaft drive replaced side chains on the company's touring range and the 7·7-litre Model 40 cost up to $5900. In 1911 came the greatest – in all senses – and most longlived of all the Locomobiles, the Model 48, a huge six which started life as a mere stripling of 7037cc, and 'just growed' to 8603cc during the course of its long production life. This 'Exclusive Car for Exclusive People' remained on the market until 1929. At their peak, Locomobile made every part of the car in their plant, including the magneto.

Peerless, who made cycles and clothes wringers in Cleveland, Ohio, in the late 1890s, had a designer of merit in Louis P. Mooers whose 1902 range, shaft-driven and with the engines in front, introduced the side-entrance tonneau to the American market, enabling the passengers in the rear seat to alight on the pavement instead of stepping out of a rear entrance on to the muddy road. Mooers was also a talented designer of racing cars; his 1903 80hp Gordon Bennett Cup car had full pressure lubrication. The same year his company brought out America's first 'off-the-peg' closed coachwork. Fitted with an 11,120cc engine and rechristened 'Green Dragon', the Gordon Bennett car, driven by the cigar-chewing racing driver Berna Eli 'Barney' Oldfield, attracted much attention at racetracks all over America, providing much valuable publicity for what had become America's most costly indigenous marque – which introduced its first six-cylinder model in 1907.

ABOVE: A late example of the Locomobile 48, the 1925 'Sportif' with an 8.6 litre engine (*Briggs Cunningham Automotive Museum. Photo: Nicky Wright*)

A second generation of American designers appeared in the years from 1910. Evidence of the changing climate of motoring in America is shown by the fact that they were best known for their sporting speedsters. These cars, devoid of all but the minimum of bodywork with two seats, a monocle windscreen and a huge bolster-shaped fuel tank, were the hallmark of the breed which helped to originate the Vaudeville joke: 'How can you tell a happy motorist? By the bugs in his teeth . . .'

The most notable of the speedster designers was Harry Stutz, who had graduated from the creation of the trendsetting American Underslung, with axles which hung below the springs, to the ownership of a company making a combined gearbox and final drive. Stutz, in order to prove his product's reliability, entered a car in the 1911 Indianapolis 500 race. The fact that it finished, even if it did not win any money, prompted Stutz to go into production under his own name with the slogan 'the Car that made good in a day'. His best-known product was the 'Bearcat' speedster. Its greatest rival was the Mercer Raceabout, the work of Finlay Robertson Porter.

These exciting and totally impracticable cars, which took little account of American road conditions and were totally useless for touring, were a reaction against the growing mediocrity of the average American car. Henry Ford had started the decline by introducing the Model T, a full-sized car at a low price, and proceeded to cut that price and swamp the market by introducing mass-production methods inspired by the Chicago pork factories. There, hogs were slaughtered and reduced to their component parts for conversion into chops, sausages and pies in a matter of minutes by the use of overhead chain conveyors. Ford's former suppliers, the Dodge Brothers, who spent their Ford dividend payments in setting up their own factory in Detroit's Polish quarter, Hamtramck, also encouraged mediocrity by adopting the body manufacturing process invented by Edward Budd who pressed coachwork from sheet steel, thus replacing the old hand methods of coachbuilding over a wooden framework.

A new breed of luxury cars, contemporary with the speedsters, were exciting for their technical innovations. Cadillac, who had blossomed under the aged Henry Leland into the technical leaders of the industry, was fortunate, as a member of General Motors, in having access to the services of Charles F. Kettering of the Dayton Engineering Laboratories Company – 'Delco' for short – who had devised a simple electrical starter which appealed to Leland whose good friend, Byron V. Carter (builder of the friction-driven Cartercar), had just been fatally injured by a starting-handle kickback. On 27 February 1911, the first Delco starter was fitted in a Cadillac and by 1912, electric lighting, and starting and battery ignition, had been standardized across the Cadillac range, setting such a trend that 'every car exhibited at the official New York Show was either equipped with an electric starter or willing to provide it if the buyer were willing to pay the added cost'. That first practical complete electrical system for a car won Cadillac a second Dewar Trophy, the only time any manufacturer has ever won this coveted award twice. Then Kettering, taking a lead from Europe where the French De Dion company had launched a production V8, introduced a 5150cc V8 Cadillac for 1915. Moreover, it had left-hand steering though fashion decreed that all cars of quality, despite the rule of the road, should have the steering on the right. Late in 1915 Peerless also brought out a V8, apparently closely modelled on the Cadillac.

Jesse G. Vincent of Packard also sought inspiration in Europe, finding it

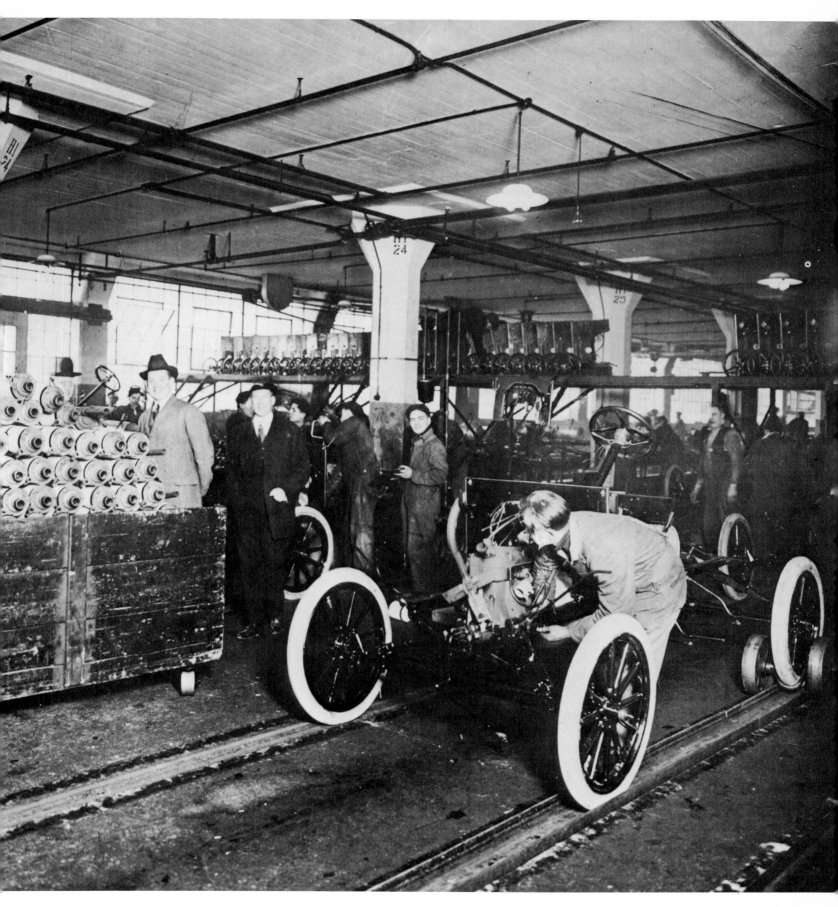

ABOVE: Henry Ford
introduced mass production
on a moving assembly line to
the motor industry and
changed the face of society
(DBW)

ABOVE: Like the American Underslung, the 1907-14 Regal Underslung's chassis passed beneath the axles (*Hillcrest Motors, Beverly Hills, California. Photo: Nicky Wright*)

instead at Sunbeam of Wolverhampton, where the Breton engineer Louis Coatalen had adapted a V12 aeroengine for racing in a car at Brooklands. The car, 'Toodles V', was shipped to America for racing and Vincent may well have seen it in the metal before creating his 1915 masterpiece, the 'Twin-Six', the world's first series-production V12, a car that was so successful that, of Packard's 1915–16 output of 18,572 cars, almost half were Twin-Sixes. The model survived in production until 1922 with a total of 35,046 being built. One of these achieved a measure of immortality by being the first car to carry a President of the United States – Warren Gamaliel Harding – to his inauguration. And, as a footnote to history, the Sunbeam-inspired Packard V12 (or, at least, a special aeroengined record-breaking version of it) was itself the inspiration for another great maker of V12 cars, Enzo Ferrari.

LEFT: The early, brass-radiatored Model T Fords like this 1914 Touring had a gauche charm (*Mr Hamilton, Fort Wayne, Ind. Photo: Nicky Wright*)

BELOW: The starkly handsome Mercer Model 35C Raceabout was perhaps America's finest sporting car (*Briggs Cunningham Automotive Museum. Photo: Nicky Wright*)

ABOVE: Henry Leland's Cadillac set the fashion to the US industry by bringing out this V8 car in 1915 (DBW)

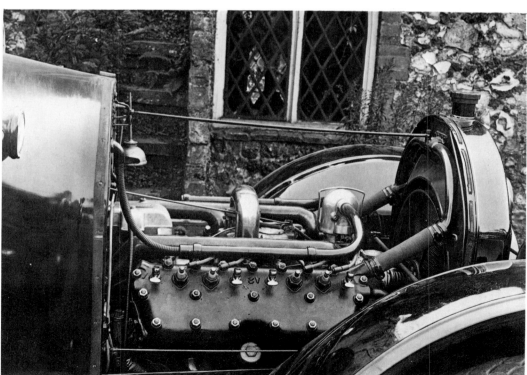

RIGHT: The 1915 Cadillac V8 engine (DBW)

America's late entry into the Great War and its isolation from the theatre of war meant that production could continue at a fair proportion of pre-war levels whereas European manufacturers had been forced to stop altogether. Already design had become stereotyped, however, and it was an expert job to distinguish between many popular models. There was as little apparent difference between a Maibohm and a Chalmers Six as there was between an Overland and a Studebaker.

Then came November 1918; the Armistice unleashed an unprecedented horde of potential car owners on to the European and American markets. Car manufacturers in both the Old World and the New braced themselves to boost output to meet the coming boom.

ABOVE: The car which inspired Packard's V12 was the Sunbeam racer *Toodles V,* seen here converted into a road car in California (DBW)

LEFT: Packard's 1915 Twin-Six was the first series production V12 car in the world: over 35,000 were built from 1915–22 (DBW)

2 No Substitute for Inches

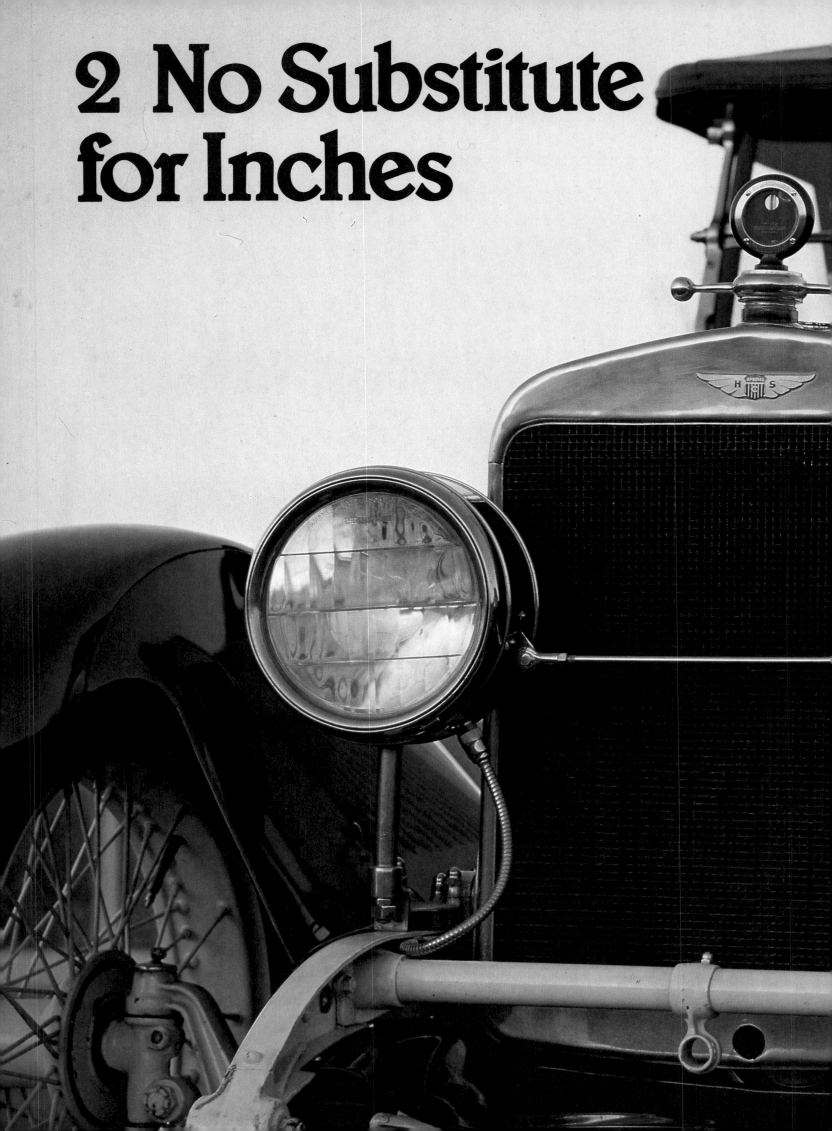

If, in 1919, four-cylinder cars seemed to predominate in the US market, this was solely due to Henry Ford who produced some 750,000 Model Ts that year. Already the four-cylinder engine was becoming the mark of the lower priced car and, of all the models in production in the United States that year, only 29 per cent were fours. Sixes represented 56 per cent while most of the remainder were V8s, with a sprinkling of V12s.

Remarkably, several of those 12s were assembled models, the American assembled car bearing none of the stigmas associated with its European counterpart – cheapness, flimsiness, or the impression of lack of financial backing. America was the home of the specialized maker of components and it was possible to assemble a high quality chassis without actually manufacturing any significant part of it. Take, for example, the Cole, a highly regarded model, which used a 40hp Northway six-cylinder engine with Delco ignition and lighting, Stromberg carburettor, Northway gearbox and Columbia rear axle, cloaking this mélange in idiosyncratic coachwork with excruciating names like 'Sportsedan', 'Sportosine', 'Tourosine' or, ultimately, 'Aero-Volante' and 'Brouette' (French for 'Wheelbarrow'). Of the fourteen or so proprietary engine makers, inevitably one – Weidely (who also offered an overhead camshaft six of advanced design) – offered a V12 as well, with its cylinders cast in blocks of three, with 90 degrees between the two banks, full pressure lubrication, Stromberg carburation and Delco dual ignition.

This power unit was on the market as early as 1917 and appeared most notably in the Highway King, a massive seven-seater offered by the Austin Automobile Company of Grand Rapids, Michigan, whose proprietor, Walter S. Austin, believed wholeheartedly in the old adage that there 'was no substitute for inches'. The long-stroke ($2\frac{7}{8} \times 5$in) Weidely, with its 6383cc swept volume, admirably suited his style. Unlike so many American cars, which offered the minimum number of forward speeds to avoid the clangorous necessity for gearchanging, the Highway King had six speeds forward and two reverse due to a dual-ratio rear axle which had long been a feature of the marque. Walter Austin, who also believed in long wheelbase to 'practically eliminate . . . the danger of skidding', was voluble, if not particularly clear, about the merits of his designs:

All claims of superior merit must be based upon a material difference in design which will show indisputable mechanical reasons why such distinctive design will give better results.

The Weidely V12 was also available in the Kissel Double-Six, an ephemeral model from a Hartford, Wisconsin, company better known for its six-cylinder speedsters. It appears to have been last listed in a catalogue, in modified form, in the 1921–22 Heine-Velox, a huge and hideous machine which, at $17,000, was the most costly American car of its time and came from a San Franciscan company that had tried (and failed) to break into the car industry once before, in 1906–09, with a mere four-cylinder of dubious reliability. The Heine-Velox V12, which boasted four-wheel hydraulic brakes – a truly advanced touch – attracted few buyers in its short life.

Even though the Weidely V12 was available there were, surprisingly, several manufacturers who preferred to concentrate on rivalling the Packard Twin-Six, though their excursions into dodecaduplicity were inevitably short and unprofitable. This is shown by the fate of the Enger Twin Six, a 1915 venture by a hitherto undistinguished Cincinnati firm which had started in 1909 making twin-cylinder high-wheelers and progressed to

PAGES 34 AND 35: The Stutz 50hp Weidely-engined sporting four (*Harrah's, Reno, Nevada. Photo: Nicky Wright*)

THE HARDING TWELVE

40 hp fours two years later. The Enger, with a modest 3904cc to its credit, lasted only until 1917; its 1916 version combined overhead valves with the dubious advantage of being capable of being operated as a six by cutting out one bank of cylinders.

Then there was Elwood Haynes of Kokomo, Indiana, who claimed (wrongly) that his horseless carriage of 1894 had been America's first. In 1916 he launched a Light Twelve which had a neat 5909cc engine with cylinders cast in two six-cylinder monoblocs set at 60 degrees; it lasted in production until 1921. Another 'own-make' V12 was the National Highway 12, a 6064cc model which was catalogued from 1916 to 1919 by a well-known Indianapolis company.

Next the HAL Twelve appeared, built by H. A. Lozier, the brother of E. R. Lozier who ran the famous Lozier car company. H. A. Lozier left the family firm in 1913 and his first 12 appeared three years later, 'distinguished by straight windshield and carpet panelling on back of front seat', replaced in September 1916 by walnut panelling. In 1917 it was noted that a new 'pocket-style tyre carrier' had been added to the specification. This handsome 6383cc model, whose prices ranged from $3600 for the tourer to $5000 for the limousine, was discontinued in 1918, only months after E. R. Lozier's company, which boasted that it made 'quality cars for quality people', had itself folded.

ABOVE: An unsuccessful attempt to break into the luxury market, the 1917 Harding Twelve had a total production of one! (*Keith Marvin*)

ABOVE: Lozier built 'quality cars for quality people' from 1905–17. This is a 1916 56hp tourer, Model 84 (*Harrah's, Reno, Nevada. Photo: Nicky Wright*)

Although those early twelve-cylinder models proved a shortlived pheno-menon, the same could not be said of the V8 which, since 1915, has always been a noteworthy feature of the American motoring scene. Once Cadillac had proved its success, the V8 quickly became a regular offering from the proprietary engine makers – Northway, Herschell-Spillman and Ferro all building V8s for the assemblers. Even Scripps-Booth, better-known for its light cars, eagerly adopted the Ferro V8, which was installed in Model D of 1916. The Ferro, incidentally, was designed by Alanson P. Brush, who liked to create engines that cranked anti-clockwise to lessen the risk of breaking one's wrist when starting the engine on the handle. Brush's name was inextricably linked with his early Brush Runabout whose axles were made of wood – 'wooden wheels, wooden axles, wooden run . . .' was how it was cruelly described.

One of the best of the 'own-make' V8s was the King Eight, 'the car of no regrets', built by Charles Brady King who had built Detroit's first motor

ABOVE: Apperson's first V8 appeared in 1914. This is the 1920 60hp Model 8-20 Four-Passenger Tourster (*Harrah's, Reno, Nevada. Photo: Nicky Wright*)

LEFT: Alongside refined light cars like this 1916 four-cylinder Model C 25hp, Scripps-Booth offered a V8 (*Harrah's, Reno, Nevada. Photo: Nicky Wright*)

RIGHT: A highly-regarded model from Philadelphia, the Murray Eight of 1916–18 was distinguished by a Rolls-Royce-like radiator (*Keith Marvin*)

BELOW: The Standard Eight was launched in 1916 by a Pittsburgh maker of railway carriages and armoured cars. This is a 1920 model (*Keith Marvin*)

VESTIBULE SEDAN

car in 1896. King was fond of quoting examples of the durability of his Eight, though one story emanating from Hong Kong and 'proving that you can't keep a good car down' did seem a trifle far-fetched. King Eight No. 6720 was shipped for European Russia *via* Vladivostok in a munition ship in 1917, and the steamer was wrecked off the China coast. After:

> *three months in salt water and eaten by corrosive acids from explosives, King car was raised and sold at auction, purchased by an English merchant (name on request) of Hong Kong who, though inexperienced mechanically, took car to pieces and reassembled. Car ran perfectly on first trial. Mr -----* says 'The engine and its parts are perfect, no car could possibly run better . . . *after three months in salt water mixed with all sorts of ammunition chemicals.*'

Another fine 'own-make' V8 was the Peerless 'Equipoised Eight', available as early as 1915, which was claimed to give the car 'second wind'. They called it the 'Two Power Range Eight' and said that it had a 'loafing' range ('to loaf along smoothly behind retarded traffic and yet be able to dash ahead the instant there is an opening . . . to have tremendous power in reserve . . . *at no expense until you use it*') and a 'sporting' range ('to take a new lease on life and climb with renewed courage when you would expect her to falter at so steep a grade . . . to speed faster and faster after you thought she had delivered her final spurt').

Slightly later, in 1920, LaFayette Motors of Mars Hill, Indianapolis, diffidently announced that their V8 was 'available for ownership'. Like the 1915 Cadillac, this car was designed by the ex-Napier engineer from England, D. McCall White; a novel feature of its specification was the use of radiator shutters. Its manufacturers advertised the car with such self-effacing diffidence that it is hardly surprising that they failed in 1923 and were acquired by the mass-producer Nash Motors, who continued the marque for a short while as their luxury line:

Now you may place your own estimate upon LaFayette. Automobiles are in the hands of our distributors and are going forth to private ownership. As you see these cars abroad upon the highways, you will have basis for comparing them with others which you admire . . . It is very possible the car will find such favour in your eyes that you will wish to own a LaFayette.

But *the* most prestigious V8 of the immediate postwar era was the Cunningham, built by the renowned carriage-building firm of James Cunningham Son & Co., of Rochester, New York, established in 1842. Beginning, in 1907, with an electric car, Cunningham soon switched to petrol ones and, by 1916, had introduced a magnificent – and costly – V8, available in funeral vehicles and ambulances as well as pleasure cars. From 1917 to 1927 the Cunningham was perhaps the most exclusive car of America with a price tag to match. Closed cars cost over $10,000 and the marque had a considerable advantage over its competitors in building its own coachwork which blended perfectly with the rounded radiator, giving the car quite a European look.

The Cunningham had perhaps one rival, the 1919 Daniels 8, built by George E. Daniels, ex-president of the Oakland car company. This boasted, after 1919, an 'own-make' 5438cc V8 engine and exquisite body styles, and its sole distinguishing mark was a letter 'D' cast in the hubcaps. 'Purposely built for people who are familiar with the highest automobile merits and will not accept less', the Daniels cost $7450 with Town Brougham coachwork, though the firm, based in Reading, Pennsylvania, was quick to point out that 'we offer no stock models – nearly every car is a special order, appealing especially to the more critical and difficult to satisfy'. The marque was, however, sold to a Philadelphia combine in 1923. Trading on the old image, they raised the price to $10,000 but failed to maintain the quality of the earlier models, and were consequently out of business by the end of 1924.

Although the V8 had become the most popular power unit for luxury automobiles, considerable stir was created by the introduction of America's first straight-eight passenger car by Fred S. Duesenberg late in 1920. The Duesenberg ('built to outclass, outrun and outlast any car on the road') had its roots in racing and aeroengine practice, for Duesenberg had operated a wartime factory at Elizabeth, New Jersey, where a number of Bugatti 16-cylinder aeroengines (basically two straight-eights in parallel with the crank shafts geared together) were built. After he sold his factory to Willys at the end of 1918, Duesenberg built straight-eight racing cars for the 1920 season plus a 16-cylinder record car, while working on the development of a straight-eight luxury car which was to be built in a new plant in Indianapolis.

The first prototypes of the Duesenberg incorporated a feature used on the racing four-cylinder engines which had previously been the company's staple peacetime product – horizontal valves operated by long 'walking beams' from a low-set camshaft; but by the time the eight reached produc-

ABOVE: 1917 Silver-Knight sporting model built on a Willys-Knight chassis by Conover T. Silver of New York (*Keith Marvin*)

tion in 1921 an overhead camshaft (perhaps inspired by the Bugatti connection?) was used. Duesenberg was also ahead of most of his contemporaries in using light alloy pistons, though prejudice from some quarters against this feature led to his offering the eight with either aluminium or cast iron pistons according to the customer's choice. Another feature well ahead of the general trend of design in America was the use of four-wheel brakes with hydraulic operation, the first time this had been seen on an American production vehicle. (Though the low-production Kenworthy Line-O-Eight, another 1920 model, also boasted four-wheel braking in conjunction with a straight-eight engine).

ABOVE: One of America's great quality cars was the Cunningham V8. This is a 1926 V6 Sport Touring (*Frank Kleptz, Terre Haute, Ind. Photo: Nicky Wright*)

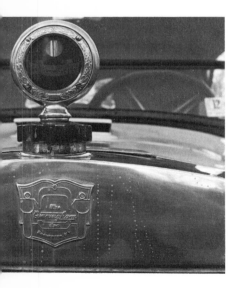

ABOVE: Hood ornament and nameplate of the 1926 Cunningham V6 Sport Touring (*Frank Kleptz, Terre Haute, Ind. Photo: Nicky Wright*)

The marque sprang to world fame in July 1921 when Jimmy Murphy won the French Grand Prix in a Duesenberg racing car with many of the touring model's features. Thereafter, the Duesenberg was sold as 'the world's champion automobile' and, in various endurance runs, proved its maker's contention that 'a Duesenberg is a thing of fineness and precision – a stress-enduring, masterful, mechanical creation – a veritable symphony in steel'. One car covered 18,032 miles in twenty-one days, another covered 3155 miles non-stop (except for two tyre changes) at 40–50mph, even taking on fuel, oil and water and relief drivers while running at speed. Both these records were achieved at the Indianapolis Speedway, which was almost permanently in use as a test track by Duesenberg.

Fred Duesenberg was, however, a far better engineer than businessman and his company was taken over in 1926 by a fast-talking ex-car salesman called Erret Lobban Cord, who was to play a crucial role in the history of the American classic car. One factor in the failure of Duesenberg was common to many makers of fine cars in the early 1920s. Because they supplied their cars in chassis form only, they were at the mercy of the coachbuilders of the day whose creations were sometimes inept – to say the least. Closed cars were especially prone to look boxy and clumsy and, on most luxury car coachwork, the finish was not markedly superior to that on cheaper mass-production models.

LEFT: The 1926 Cunningham
V6 Sport Touring, showing
the engine (*Frank Kleptz,
Terre Haute, Ind. Photo:
Nicky Wright*)

RIGHT: This magnificent
sports-touring car is the 1919–
20 Cunningham Model V3,
with an own-make V8 power
unit (*Keith Marvin*)

BELOW: This 1922 Daniels
5438cc four-passenger sedan
was built to the order of Mr
Joseph Hyman of New York
(*Keith Marvin*)

Perhaps the most salutary example of how a proud company could be brought down by the appearance of its cars was the story of Lincoln, originally founded in 1917 by Henry M. Leland who had resigned from Cadillac (which had become part of General Motors in 1909) in order to build Liberty aeroengines, taking with him just the superlative engineering skills that had earned him the nickname 'Master of Precision' and a factory site. Seven months later the first of a contracted order for 6000 engines was running and, within ten months, a workforce of 6000 was producing fifty engines a day. Leland chose the name 'Lincoln', incidentally, because of his boyhood hero, Abraham Lincoln, for whom he had cast his first vote in the 1860s.

The end of the war came too soon for Leland; in another six months he could have built sufficient engines to pay off his bank and government loans but the cessation of orders for aeroengines meant that he had to change tack and find another use for his factory. He decided to return to the manufacture of luxury cars and, on 26 January 1920, founded a new company, Lincoln Motor Company of Delaware, which took over the old firm's property, business and other assets, plus some of its Government debts. The company attracted investments worth $6.5 million but, with an old man's obstinacy, Leland (he was fast approaching eighty) insisted that his company should be equipped with the very best machine tools available and spent all the money in eight months. With 1000 orders registered for the new – and as yet unbuilt – Lincoln car, Leland had to borrow a further $3.7 million to get into production. He made much of the 'literally thousands upon thousands of devices, tools and gauges employed to ensure Leland standards of precision', yet most of the Lincoln car, apart from its 5·8-litre engine, was, in fact, assembled from proprietary components – axles, gears, brakes, chassis and ignition, while the bodies, though company-designed, were also from outside suppliers.

The design of those early Lincoln bodies also attracted fierce criticism. It was claimed, with fair justification, that they were lacking in style. They had been designed by Angus Woodbridge, Leland's son-in-law, whose qualifications as a car stylist rested on his former experience as a milliner. Even more damning than the ineptness of these milliner-bodied models was the claim by Walter Wagner, who bought machinery and checked gauges for the Lincoln Company, that the chief inspector, Archer (on whom the final quality control depended), seemed to have been chosen because he had a fine speaking voice and sang in Leland's church choir. 'He couldn't tell a gauge from a washboard,' said Wagner.

Such allegations worried some of Leland's backers, notably Dr Fred T. Murphy whose uncle, William H. Murphy, had been the principal investor in the original Cadillac company. A minor lull in sales caused by a sudden and unexpected slump in the US car industry which brought the euphoric postwar boom to an end gave Murphy ammunition for his contentions and he disagreed strongly with Leland, who exulted in September 1920: 'We've turned the corner – from now on it's forward!'

Both the company treasurer, Henry Nash, and the man who had put the company stock on the market, G. Hermann Kinnicut, supported Leland's view, arguing that the company was basically sound and needed only a modest cash injection to return it to viability. Murphy insisted that the company should be totally refinanced. When Henry Leland and his son Wilfred failed to raise a large loan in November 1921, nemesis struck two days later (aided, claimed Wilfred Leland, by Murphy, who wanted

OPPOSITE: The Model A Duesenberg had a 4261cc overhead camshaft straight-eight engine (*Homer Fitterling, Auburn-Cord-Duesenberg Museum. Photo: Nicky Wright*)

ABOVE: The Model A Duesenberg, showing the hood ornament and name-plate (*Homer Fitterling, Auburn-Cord-Duesenberg Museum. Photo : Nicky Wright*)

ABOVE RIGHT: Fred S. Duesenberg who, with his brother August, created the straight-eight Duesenbergs of the 1920s and 1930s (*Auburn-Cord-Duesenberg Museum*)

complete control of the company). The Lelands received a huge bill from the Government, mostly in respect of alleged underpayment of tax which later proved (when it was too late) to have been issued in error. The Murphy faction produced evidence that the company was running at a loss and applied for it to be put into receivership, with the apparent aim of acquiring Lincoln at a bargain price.

The Lelands opposed the receivership, and steadfastly claimed that they would buy the company themselves, revitalize it, and pay off the creditors and stockholders. But they lacked the finance to do this and took the less attractive alternative of trying to find a buyer who would take over Lincoln yet allow them the complete autonomy in its running that they sought.

They approached Henry Ford, who had previously shown some slight interest in Lincoln (he had used their aeroengines in the Eagle submarine chaser boats he had built, on a moving production line, to aid the war effort). Unfortunately, when they met, Ford failed to give the Lelands a definite assurance that he would put up the money. Disappointed, the Lelands left Ford's rambling home, Fair Lane. As the door closed behind them, Clara Ford (Henry called her his 'Helper' as she was such a dominant influence on him) chided her husband. 'Can't you do anything to help them? It's a shame that all Detroit should stand by and see that company wrecked.'

Henry's 28-year-old son Edsel was keen on buying Lincoln as well for he saw it as an outlet for the frustration he felt in being unable to see his ideas on styling put into production. His father was extremely reluctant to change the homely appearance of the Model T and hitherto Edsel had had to be content with one-off custom models based on modified Model T chassis. Tired of living the life of a crown prince, Edsel Ford wanted to break new ground. Playing golf with a friend at one of the exclusive clubs established in Detroit for the executives of the motor industry, Edsel sighed: 'Father makes the most popular car in the world . . . I should like to make the best car.' Edsel and Clara discussed the possibility of a Ford takeover of Lincoln and secured the agreement of a number of Ford's top management; when they told Henry, he replied: 'Tell the Lelands to come out and talk it over.'

By December 1921 it was all settled; Ford would provide the money necessary to save Lincoln. The promise of help from such a strong source must have scared off the Murphy faction for, at the receivership sale in February 1922, Ford's bid was the only one – a healthy offer of $8 million. Henry Ford insisted that the management of the Lincoln and Ford companies would remain 'separate and distinct' (though Edsel joined Wilfred Leland as a Vice President of Lincoln), but it soon became apparent that the two Henrys were incapable of working together. Under Edsel's guidance, the old, stolid body styles were phased out and more attractive models introduced, prices were slashed, and Ford staff put into Lincoln to see where the company could be made more efficient. Orders worth $2 million were taken but Leland was unhappy. He resented the presence of the Ford men in what he still regarded as his factory and resisted any suggestion that production methods should be changed. There was growing hostility between Ford and Leland and Wilfred Leland apparently approached Henry Ford to see if he would sell the company back to its founders.

'Mr Leland,' said Henry in a matter-of-fact voice, 'I wouldn't sell the Lincoln plant for $500 million.' And by mid June 1922 the Lelands had been given their marching orders and Edsel was in sole command. Production processes were rationalized, limited use made of conveyor-belt assembly

LEFT: A *c*1924 Lincoln Phaeton heading a parade of Ford cars in Phoenix Park, Dublin, Ireland, in 1927 (DBW)

49

and a range of series-produced custom coachwork introduced. Obstinacy had cost Henry Leland his company, yet none of the standards he revered had been compromised by the Ford ownership. The cars were built to even closer tolerances and certainly the association benefited the mass-produced Ford cars in many ways.

About the same time that Henry Leland was creating the first Lincoln, McFarlan, an old-established firm from Connersville, Indiana, was enjoying its greatest success with its most famous model. McFarlan had its origins in the McFarlan carriage works established in the 1850s, on a site that was to become one of America's first industrial estates. Since they had begun building cars in 1909, McFarlan had become known for the quality – and variety – of the coachwork they offered. Their model names included 'Submarine' (a sports phaeton), 'Pasadena' (a five-passenger touring car), 'Knickerbocker Cabriolet' and 'Philadelphia Brougham'. Production was always small and the six-cylinder engines that were specially built for the make always large. In 1917 the company had launched a Teetor-engined 'Ninety' of 9381cc with such luxury features as an electrically heated steering wheel and, in 1917, a 'magnetic' gearchange, with gears shifted electrically and controlled by push-buttons. (This should not be confused with the 'magnetic' transmission devised by Ray M. Baker around 1914, which interposed a dynamo between engine and final drive to give 'a thousand speeds').

In 1920 the Ninety's successor appeared, the Twin Valve Six, whose power unit was built in Dayton, Ohio, at the workshop of the company's consulting engineer, Jesse Kepler. Its engine capacity was identical to its predecessor and this huge car was the biggest McFarlan built so far, riding on a 140-in wheelbase. Its power unit developed a healthy 120 brake horsepower and was equipped with twenty-four valves and eighteen spark plugs (supplied by a single coil ignition system and a twin-spark magneto). The McFarlan had a speed range of 3 to 76mph on top gear and was said to be the most powerful six-cylinder car on the American market. The only car to exceed it in this respect was the ephemeral Porter, of which a total of thirty-four were built between 1919 and 1922. The designer of this $10,000 four-cylinder was Finlay Robertson Porter, late of Mercer.

The McFarlan, as well as increasing in power, moved sharply upmarket with prices rising by $1300 to $2500 across the range. The Knickerbocker Cabriolet, for example, an ornate machine with *six* mudguards (two to protect the rear step from splashes), opera lamps, and oval windows to the rear and sides of the fabric covered rear quarter, rose from $6500 on the Ninety chassis to $9000 on the new TV chassis, an increase of 27.7 per cent. To emphasize the new status of the marque as the eighth most expensive car on the American market, the McFarlan acquired a tall, angular radiator shell which rose $1\frac{1}{2}$in above the level of the bonnet. McFarlan kept to its high prices during 1921 when most other manufacturers cut prices in an attempt to maintain sales in an economic recession and saw sales of the new model slump to only eighty-five, against 210 for the previous model in 1920 but, in 1922, sales rose to the marque's all-time best of 235 cars.

A marque of similar antecedents to McFarlan was Velie of Moline, Illinois. By coincidence it entered the car market in 1909 after over forty years in the carriage-building trade but built only fours until 1915 when the 'Biltwell Model 22', with a 40hp Continental six-cylinder engine, appeared. Velie cars were, it seems, so popular in Shreveport, Louisiana, that a suburb of the town was named Velie in 1916. Two years later came

ABOVE: When Harry Stutz left Stutz in 1919, he founded HCS, building a 50hp Weidely-engined sporting four (*Harrah's, Reno, Nevada. Photo : Nicky Wright*)

the most distinctive Velie, the marvellously impracticable Sport Car, a 4966cc six with triple outside exhausts and a Victoria hood which protected only the rear seat passengers. In the 1920s Velie lowered their standards and their prices and the lines of their cars became more angular, a move which earned the marque the unfortunate nicknames of 'the connoisseur's clunker . . . the ugly duckling of the prairies'. Nevertheless Velie, having adopted a policy diametrically opposed to that of McFarlan, had precisely the same life-span, both marques expiring in 1928.

While it was feasible for small companies rooted in coachbuilding tradition – like McFarlan or Velie – to offer individual bodywork on their own chassis, other firms took standard production quality cars and modified them to suit the taste (and the bank balance) of wealthy customers. Such a car was the 'Uppercu Cadillac', modified about 1924 by a leading agent of the marque, Inglis Uppercu, to resemble a cross between a Rolls-Royce and a McFarlan. Another company, Pease, took a Packard Twin-Six, lengthened the chassis and fitted a 'Rolls-Royce' radiator.

The philosophy of the early customizers was well expressed by Charles Schutte, a coachbuilder from Lancaster, Pennsylvania, who advertised in 1922:

Whether a Dashing Speedster of Rakish Design, or an Ultra Conservative Cabriolet of Plainest Lines, Schutte Creations possess that Atmosphere of Individuality, that Intangible Something which distinguishes them from other *Automobiles. Our Facilities include the Mounting of a Radiator of Exclusive Pattern, the Alteration of the Entire External Appearance, as well as the Shortening or Lengthening of the chassis.*

There was a very strong market for such 'customized' vehicles on the West Coast, especially in California, where the growth of the film industry and the creation of the star system had brought great prosperity to the region. Many of those made newly wealthy by films wanted to flaunt their status by driving unique motor cars. One was the comedian Roscoe 'Fatty' Arbuckle who, in the early 1920s, shortly before he was engulfed in the

RIGHT: The mighty McFarlan Twin Valve Six roadster had a 120hp power unit. This 1921 roadster sold for $6300 (*Keith Marvin*)

The McFarlan Six roadster, $6,300

BELOW: Finlay Robertson Porter, creator of the Mercer Raceabout, designed the 1919–22 Porter six-cylinder luxury car (*Keith Marvin*)

PORTER

Limousine
Body Style S

scandal caused by the death of a starlet named Virginia Rappe at a party at an hotel, owned a McFarlan Knickerbocker Cabriolet. Arbuckle had acquired this impressive car when its original owner, Wallace Reid, a hero of the silent dramas of the day (with eloquent titles like 'My Lips Betray') had died from drug abuse, although Arbuckle was known best for his customized Pierce-Arrow which was disguised by a new radiator and wheels.

A leading supplier of such customized vehicles was the Don Lee Corporation of Los Angeles which, after the First World War, had acquired the Earl Carriage Works, an old-established company which had been coachbuilders and carriage makers for many years. The son of the company's founder was a young man named Harley J. Earl, born late in 1893, who had been educated in the private schools of California and at Leland Stanford University. He had received the basics of a sound training and practical experience of the coachbuilding industry, including designing and drafting, in his father's factory.

When the Don Lee Corporation took over, young Harley stayed on as director, having shown a remarkable talent for designing customized car bodies on both foreign and American chassis. He created both open and closed bodies, and earned 'an enviable reputation' as an automobile designer. While working for Don Lee, Harley Earl made his first contact with Cadillac in Detroit and was eventually to be retained by them as a consulting engineer. It was the start of a relationship that was to prove crucial to the history of the American classic car.

ABOVE: Customizers could transform quite mundane cars, like this 1919 Essex, into dashing speedsters of rakish appearance (DBW)

3 The Jazz Age

Henry Ford lost no time in letting the world know that he was in sole command at Lincoln. Press reports on the revised car appearing at the end of June 1922 called it the 'Ford-Lincoln' and admired its 'elegant and graceful lines'.

The 1922 Lincoln was full of ingenious ideas: it had an 'electro fog generator' linked to the choke which automatically heated the intake manifold in cold weather by means of an electric element and its cooling system was sealed 'to prevent the necessity of refilling the water system and also to prevent the loss of expensive anti-freezing solutions should they be required'; the float rod that recorded the depth of oil in the sump ended in a luminous ball that could be seen by night as well as day; dipping headlights (a rarity at the period) were standard; there was a tyre pump in unit with the gearbox, and the steering wheel was hinged so that corpulent drivers could get into the seat more easily.

T. J. Litle, the company's chief engineer, boasted proudly that the cars were made to such close tolerances that they required no running in. A range of standard bodywork, styled by Brunn, 'of distinctly European outline' was offered, while there was also a range of custom coachwork from LeBaron, Willoughby, Judkins, Locke and Dietrich.

Lincoln produced 7875 cars in the 1923–24 season and was showing a profit for the first time by 1924. Evidence of the company's improved status was given by the adoption of the Lincoln as an official car by President Calvin Coolidge. Lincolns were built to a very high standard despite the fact that, under the new regime, an exchange engine for a Lincoln could be obtained for as little as $100 and parts were interchangeable between old and new cars (just like the humble Model T Ford) Every car, whether fitted with standard or custom coachwork, was submitted to searching tests before it was released from the factory.

The Lincoln was the first, and arguably the best, of the so-called 'volume classics'. These were quality cars which, although built in quantity, were equal or superior to the esoteric obscurities made in tiny numbers. In 1928 the Lincoln engine was increased in swept volume to 6.3 litres and the crankshaft fitted with counterweights to improve the sweetness of running. This was a very fine car indeed. In the mid 1960s I was fortunate enough to be able to road-test a 1929 Lincoln which had once belonged to a director of Ford in Britain, a massive maroon saloon weighing about 5190lb. It anticipated the modern trend for hatchbacks by having a fifth door at the rear where the original owner's wife, who was an invalid, could be helped into the car in her wheelchair. Very much a top-gear car, the Lincoln could be throttled down to run at a walking pace (when it seemed that you could almost count the beats of that beautiful V8 engine) and yet still accelerate away smoothly, without skipping a beat, right up to a healthy maximum speed. The big surprise was the steering, which was light and effortless to use though somewhat devoid of feel, and very much like that of a modern car.

Packard was also keenly involved in the volume market, having introduced a six alongside the V12 in 1921. This 'Single Six' was intended to be Packard's popular model and 8800 were built in 1921–22. But the big news from Packard was the dropping of the Twin-Six in June 1923; its place was taken by the Single Eight, which introduced the straight-eight configuration to series production. Displacing 5860cc, the Single Eight was only 6bhp less powerful than the 6950cc Twin-Six and was available with a wheelbase of either 136in or 143in. Prices ranged from $3850 for the Runabout to

LEFT: Here fitted to a 1920
Kissel from the Harrah
Museum, the 'fat man' tilting
steering wheel was also fitted
to 1922 Lincolns (*Harrah's,
Reno, Nevada. Photo: Nicky
Wright*)

BELOW: This elegant Packard
Eight town car was discovered
in Portugal in the mid 1970s.
Beside it is a 1930 Cadillac V8
convertible (DBW)

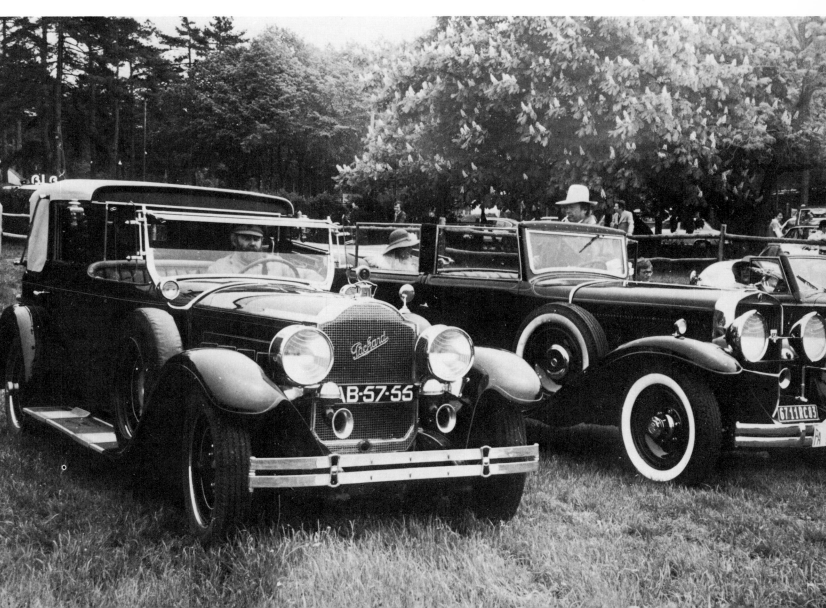

$4950 for the long wheelbase Limousine.

The chassis featured front wheel brakes and was America's first series-production car with brakes on all four wheels though, initially, these were of the external-contracting pattern which were totally useless in wet conditions. The eight also had a four-speed gearbox, another feature counter to the prevailing American trend, which usually required three-speed transmissions. Alvan Macauley, the former patent lawyer who headed Packard, was justifiably proud of the new car:

> *The Eight in its standard form is equipped with every luxury and embellishment the markets of the world afford . . . The broadcloths, silks and fabrics with which the body is trimmed are the finest obtainable. In order to cater to the wishes of an exacting clientèle, which often desires bodies built to respond to some unusual personal preferences, we offer a complete line of custom bodies. We have not sought quantity in connection with the Eight. We think it best to keep it on a plane where it will always be in demand and where in normal times the demand will be somewhat greater than the supply.*

Macaulay, incidentally, had come to Packard from the Burroughs Adding Machine Company in 1910. He brought Jesse Vincent with him, whom he had noticed as a 20-year-old toolmaker and a 'very clever mechanic'. Vincent 'had had no engineering experience, but showed such marked industry and talent that Macaulay had him transferred to the engineering department. Within a few months, he was acting as chief engineer.' Thus this untrained adding machine mechanic had become one of the most noted automotive engineers in America.

The success of the volume classics was due to the custom coachbuilders who were prepared to adapt to the techniques of mass production. They clothed their chassis in elegant bodywork which was built in sufficient numbers to bring down the unit cost while still maintaining a high degree of exclusiveness. Lincoln, for instance, would order bodies that appealed to Edsel Ford in lots of a hundred or more.

The young designers with progressive ideas, which Edsel appreciated, came mainly from New York studios and often had 'working arrangements' with coachbuilding companies who were prepared to build bodies for them once an order had been secured. The designer would sketch out a particularly appealing styling idea and present it 'on spec' to a rich prospective client. If the client liked it and placed an order, the stylist would then have it built for him on the chassis of his choice; if the client thought it too extreme but found that the idea of having a bespoke motor car built for him appealing, the stylist then had an excellent chance to secure the commission.

Ray Dietrich was one of the most distinguished of the 'New York School' stylists. He started with the Brewster company of New York (which dated back to 1810) as a draughtsman and designer earning nine to twelve dollars a week, which could mean working sixty, seventy-two or even eighty hours 'learning the body business from the ground up'. Dietrich, whose motto was: 'If you can't originate, don't try to copy', subsequently went into partnership with two other young artists, Ralph Roberts and Tom Hibbard. Though all three were American, they called their partnership 'LeBaron' as they thought the name had 'an intriguing foreign sound that helped to attract customers, since the most glamorous cars of the day were imported European customs'.

LeBaron chose well-known coachbuilders like Derham, Fleetwood,

Locke, United Holbrook and the Bridgeport Body Company to build bodies from their renderings. Feeling that a genuine European connection would also help their sales, LeBaron sent Tom Hibbard to Paris in 1923 to open a branch office. LeBaron had already had a representative, Howard 'Dutch' Darrin, in 'la Ville Lumière' since 1922, and the two men managed to secure orders for custom coachwork on chassis such as Hispano-Suiza and Isotta-Fraschini. The prestige that LeBaron gained from these commissions reflected on their business in America where Locomobile and Stearns-Knight ordered LeBaron coachwork for their chassis. By now LeBaron was so successful that it needed its own body plant to handle the volume of orders that were pouring in and consequently merged with the Bridgeport Body Company, of Bridgeport, Connecticut.

Next came the first order from Lincoln in 1924. Edsel Ford and Ray Dietrich found they had much in common and became firm friends. Edsel was so impressed with the work of LeBaron that he attempted to persuade Ray Dietrich to move the company to Detroit. Ralph Roberts, however, refused to move. He argued that to transfer LeBaron to Detroit would mean an inevitable loss of personality. Dietrich reluctantly sold his share in LeBaron and moved to Detroit in 1925 where Edsel, who had a financial interest in the Murray Body Corporation, had suggested to the Murray Board that they should put up 50 per cent of the capital needed to establish Dietrich, Inc., which started business on Clay Street, Detroit, working mainly for Lincoln and Packard. After two years the company decided that it needed larger premises; Edsel therefore enabled Ray Dietrich to buy the old Leland Lincoln plant on Hamilton and Holden Avenues at a very advantageous price.

Dietrich's move left Ralph Roberts in a quandary. Roberts knew the LeBaron company intimately but had never designed a body (he was the partner who had been responsible for the day-to-day running of the company). How could he maintain LeBaron's reputation for style without a recognized designer (Hibbard had also dropped out of the company) and keep the Bridgeport factory in full operation? It seems that Roberts, however, though he did not know the technique of body designing, at least had a connoisseur's eye for stylish coachwork. He solved the problem by

ABOVE LEFT: The Winton six-cylinder sedan (*Contemporary illus.* Vogue, *1920*)

The Franklin sedan (*Contemporary illus.* Vogue, *1920*)

The National six-cylinder touring car (*Contemporary illus.* Vogue, *1920*)

BELOW RIGHT: Moon's Victory model (*Contemporary illus.*, Vogue, *1920*)

BELOW LEFT: Milburn electric coupé (*Contemporary illus.*, Vogue, *1920*)

BELOW RIGHT: The six-cylinder Moline-Knight (*Contemporary illus.*, Vogue, *1920*)

'dictating' new designs to a staff artist, Roland Stickney, who drew the design while Ralph Roberts described what the body should look like.

The technique certainly worked. In 1928 the Briggs Body Corporation was looking for a 'name' coachbuilding subsidiary to compete with Murray (who had Dietrich), and General Motors (whose Fisher Body subsidiary had bought Fleetwood in 1925) and they made Ralph Roberts an offer. This time he could not refuse to move his business to Detroit. The LeBaron headquarters therefore moved to Detroit and the New York office transferred uptown to Fifth Avenue. Among LeBaron's Detroit customers were Lincoln, Packard, Pierce-Arrow and Stutz.

BELOW LEFT: A five-passenger Victoria ReVere (*Contemporary illus.*, Vogue, *1920*)

BELOW RIGHT: Packard touring-car with a Brooks-Ostruk body (*Contemporary illus.*, Vogue, *1920*)

BOTTOM: McFarlan six-cylinder sedan (*Contemporary illus.*, Vogue, *1920*)

The third partner in the original LeBaron company, Tom Hibbard, had broken away to set up an independent company in Paris in partnership with 'Dutch' Darrin. The Hibbard & Darrin company was organized with 'practically no financial backing' but obviously plenty of wit. They discovered that the prestigious Belgian marque Minerva had no Paris agency. Employing similar tactics to those they had used in New York, they made up strikingly dramatic designs based on the 32/34hp Minerva chassis and sold 'orders' from these paper dreams (even though they had no chassis to sell) and then took these 'orders' to Minerva in Antwerp where their sheer cheek secured them the Parisian agency!

One of the most spectacular designs produced by the Hibbard & Darrin studios was an eye-catching low-slung cabriolet on the Minerva chassis for the Belgian ex-Premier Paul van Zeeland. This appeared to be almost entirely bonnet, with tiny slits of windows and about as much forward vision as a Schneider Trophy seaplane – a windscreen like a glazed letterbox.

Dietrich and his LeBaron partners had achieved fame in a very short space of time but there were also influential custom coachbuilders whose reputation had been painstakingly built up over several generations. Such a firm was Derham of Rosemont, a couple of miles east of Philadelphia. Its founder, Joseph J. Derham, was a wheelwright who had emigrated from Ireland in 1882, at the age of fifteen, to work for a Philadelphia blacksmith named Ned Wiles, who built carriages as a sideline. After five years Derham joined another blacksmith, Thomas Ryan, in Rosemont. Derham designed and made carriage bodies for which Ryan made the metal fittings, and established an enviable reputation as a carriage builder. His two-wheeled Meadowbrooks, landaus, broughams and phaetons had such a name for quality that even his former employer, Wiles, happily gave up his job to work for Derham.

Joseph Derham was innately conservative and aloofly ignored the advent of the motor car so that the company did not build its first car body until 1907, and even then with reluctance. One of their regular customers had bought a car and wanted to use it during the winter. He therefore asked Derham to build him a closed body so that he could drive in comfort through snow and rain. It was so successful that Derham received orders for similar coachwork from other customers which, in due course and again seemingly reluctantly, he executed. Horse carriages were still the company's mainstay, however, when Derham's four sons – Joseph Jr., James, Enos and Philip – started work there in 1910–12. Joseph Jr. was responsible for body design; Philip was in charge of coordination of production and sales while James worked in the sales and administration departments. Joseph Jr. died unexpectedly so Enos, the youngest son, had to leave college and take his place.

Gradually automobile bodies came to supplant horse carriages, and Derham opened a second plant in Philadelphia in 1916 to supply batches of 'semi-custom' bodies to Packard's New York and Philadelphia branches. Packard's New York manager, Grover Forrest, had conceived the idea of a 'custom body department' so that the cars could be sold as a complete bespoke package rather than in chassis form only (and, of course, that also meant that Packard could make a mark-up profit on the bodywork supplied through them). Forrest's successor, Parvis, convinced Alvan Macauley that this was the right policy for the entire Packard organization to follow. By 1926 Packard was Derham's largest customer for semi-custom bodies and the company was earning about $800,000 annually from its custom coach

ABOVE: Wheel from the 1927 Lincoln Model L-134B (*Harrah's, Reno, Nevada. Photo: Nicky Wright*)

RIGHT: Judkins built the anachronistic 'Coaching Brougham' body on this 1927 Lincoln Model L-134B (*Harrah's, Reno, Nevada. Photo: Nicky Wright*)

BELOW: 1923 Auburn Beauty-Six Formal Sedan displays the lack of style which hampered sales (*Auburn-Cord-Duesenberg Museum. Photo: Nicky Wright*)

work. As demand grew, the Rosemont factory grew organically to meet it, a modern two-storey plant springing up round the nucleus of old James's carriage works.

Brunn & Co. was an even older-established firm than Derham and was founded in 1908 in Buffalo, New York, by Hermann A. Brunn on the basis of a family involvement of more than fifty years in the carriage-building trade. Hermann Brunn, described as a 'rare combination of stylist and engineer', specialized in building custom coachwork on imported chassis and among his hallmarks were the use of a tonneau windshield and the introduction of the metal 'top boot' to conceal the folded hood of an open car within the bodywork. He also designed a pillarless two-door coupé. Brunn was heavily committed to building bodies for Lincoln in the 1920s – Brunn coachwork was said to be Edsel Ford's favourite personal choice even though the firm had been commissioned to provide coachwork for the original Leland Lincolns which were not renowned for their elegance.

Edsel Ford also came to the rescue of another well-known custom body builder around this time. Willoughby & Co. had been established in Utica, New York, in 1914. By the early 1920s it was supplying Cole, Marmon, Locomobile and Studebaker but, as the market changed, Willoughby's customers either went out of business or stopped buying custom bodywork. The loss of orders was traumatic for Willoughby, who combined the traditional skills of panelling aluminium over an iron-reinforced ash frame with the advanced technique of employing aluminium castings for windscreen pillars, rear quarters and door framing. Finally, of all Willoughby's former customers, only Locomobile and Rolls-Royce of America were left. Then Edsel Ford stepped in with an order for Lincoln bodies that put Willoughby back in action and helped it to attract new customers.

As the 1920s jazzed their way along, it seemed that the custom coach-builders could supply bodywork to suit every mood and taste. The 1927

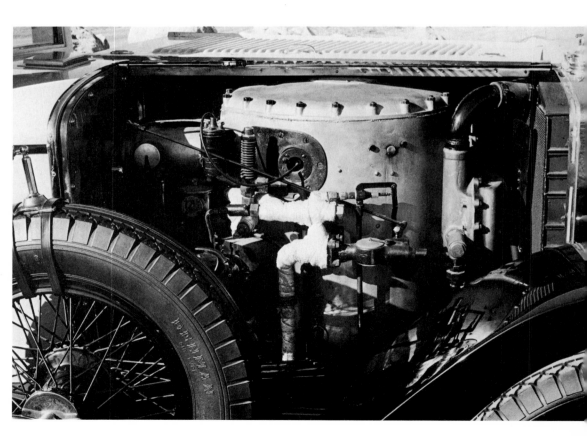

RIGHT: Detail of the 1925 Doble Series E (*Harrah's, Reno, Nevada. Photo: Nicky Wright*)

Lincoln catalogue, for instance, 'graphically presented the various periods of art and history that had inspired the designers in their choice of interiors, trims and fittings'. A LeBaron coupé, it was claimed, had an Oriental theme with trimming in 'rich gold, black and sunburst red'. The recurrent 1920s Egyptian inspiration could be seen in a Judkins Berline, which had 'lotus blossoms and papyrus etched in needlepoint', Judkins also offered a 'Coaching Brougham' that year. An example of this vehicle – which harked back to the days of the stagecoach – still survives in the amazing Harrah Collection in Reno, Nevada. 'Hand-carved window garnitures' on a Willoughby Limousine were said to reflect a 'Gothic influence' and Willoughby also presented a Colonial Cabriolet whose 'antique charm' sprang from the use of broadcloth trim 'woven in bellflower pattern'. The ubiquitous Ray Dietrich offered a choice of 'Roman' inspiration on a Club Roadster with ribbed broadcloth interior, or ultra-modern, in the shape of a Dual-Cowl Boat-tail Roadster trimmed in two-tone green hand-crushed leather with orange piping.

These delightful bodies unquestionably contributed to the tremendous success of the Lincoln in the mid 1920s. Even more striking, perhaps, was the effect of the introduction of decently styled bodywork on the Auburn range. Even though the company used a peacock as a symbolic frame for their advertising, the 'Beauty-Six' of the early 1920s was a somewhat leaden device which accurately reflected the Auburn company's stuffy boast that its 'business policy had always been conducted on the solid platform of "keeping both feet on the ground"'. Production of the Beauty-Six had crumbled to six a day by 1924 and 700 unsold cars were establishing squatters' rights on the company lot. In desperation the company appointed one of America's top car salesmen, the 30-year-old Erret Lobban Cord, as general manager on his own terms with a share in the company and the chance to buy the controlling interest if his plans to revitalise Auburn were successful.

A vigorous sales campaign cleared the unsold Beauty-Sixes from the inventory while the company's chief engineer, James Crawford, designed a new chassis around an eight-in-line Lycoming which first appeared early in 1925. The Lycoming engine, built to Auburn specifications, incorporated such refinements as semi-automatic spark advance and a force-feed pressure lubrication system controlled by the opening of the throttle. Designed for durability, the 6-in section chassis frame was braced by seven cross-members and suspended on multi-leaf semi-elliptic springs specially constructed for smooth riding. Redesigned for 1926, the Auburn eight was increased in capacity from 276 to 298.6 cu. in, and redesignated '8–88'. The coachwork offered included a snappy roadster whose rumble (dickey) seat had a side door for easier access and a 2–3 passenger coupé covered in Meritas fabric. Closed models had fixed Brewster-style sun visors while a neat styling trick, which was to become a feature of most Auburns, was a belt line which swept up on to the bonnet and came to a point behind the radiator cap thus forming a distinctive dividing line for two-tone paintwork.

Auburn prospered greatly under Cord's direction. He increased sales of 2500 cars in 1924 to 15,000 in 1927 and converted a loss of almost $70,000 in the former year into a profit of over $1 million in the latter. By that time he had become President of Auburn and had also taken control of Duesenberg, which had just been reorganized after being put into receivership. Cord intended to use Duesenberg to build the world's most expensive passenger car. At first the two companies were run as separate entities but the million dollar profits that Auburn made in 1926 and 1927 enabled Auburn to buy the overall control of Duesenberg. The two companies were then welded together as the nucleus of the engineering empire that Cord planned. He also added to them the Lycoming Company of Williamsport, Pennsylvania (who made Auburn's engines) and the Limousine Body Company of Kalamazoo, Michigan, who had been building Auburn bodies to the design of the Walter M. Murphy Company of Pasadena, California.

Murphy had started as a West Coast distributor for Leland Lincolns but he found that their dull appearance was not popular with his Hollywood clientèle. He failed to convince old H. M. Leland to redesign so he took matters into his own hands. Murphy bought the Healey Body Company from its founder, Colonel Healey, and moved it to Pasadena where he added eye-catching new paintwork and some mild customizing to all the Lincolns shipped to California. This venture became unnecessary with the Ford takeover of Lincoln so Murphy took the natural step of building custom bodywork on luxury chassis for the fashion leaders of the movie industry.

This proved to be an excellent way of advertising his work and Murphy was soon being called in as a styling consultant by the leading car manufacturers. He was asked to build prototypes for Peerless, Stutz, Franklin and Packard among others, but among his most famous designs of the 1920s were the convertible sedan and convertible coupé for Auburn. These were in production for five years without major change and represented 50 per cent of total automobile production in that period. The job was subcontracted to Kalamazoo, however, because of the large numbers of bodies involved and the difficulty of shipping them the thousands of miles from California to Indiana.

For every Erret Lobban Cord figure who arrived on the scene to save a failing company, there were also plenty who saw their dreams of success crumble before their eyes. One of these was Childe Harold Wills, the

brilliant metallurgist whose engineering skills had been a major factor in the success of the Ford Motor Company. He and Henry Ford had been finding it increasingly difficult to agree on company policy. Henry Ford stubbornly refused to listen to anyone who tried to tell him that the demand for the Model T was finite and that a successor should be developed. In March 1919 Wills had resigned, taking with him severance pay totalling $1,592,128.39. 'I am anxious to do something worthwhile,' Wills told the press, 'and this seems the opportune time to start.'

Wills' plan included turning 4400 acres at Marysville, Michigan, into a model industrial community and developing a car that would be ten years ahead of its time. His Wills Sainte Claire, named after Lake Ste. Claire, a local beauty spot, appeared in 1921. It was hailed as a 'metallurgical masterpiece'.

'Why is the Wills Sainte Claire universally acclaimed the year's outstanding triumph in motor car design and construction?' demanded Wills's advertising.

Because of the marvellously smooth eight-cylinder 60-degree engine, because of overhead valve and camshaft construction, because of the elimination of chains, belts and other obsolete practices and the general simplification of design . . . Because of mo-lyb-den-um super steel, which unites lightness of weight with new durability, riding comfort and the security of great strength

ABOVE: 1927 Auburn 6-66/ Wanderer Sedan, bodied by McFarlan, showing how E. L. Cord restyled the Auburn (*Mrs P. Jordan, Auburn-Cord-Duesenberg Museum. Photo: Nicky Wright*)

ABOVE: E. L. Cord (*Auburn-Cord-Duesenberg Museum*)

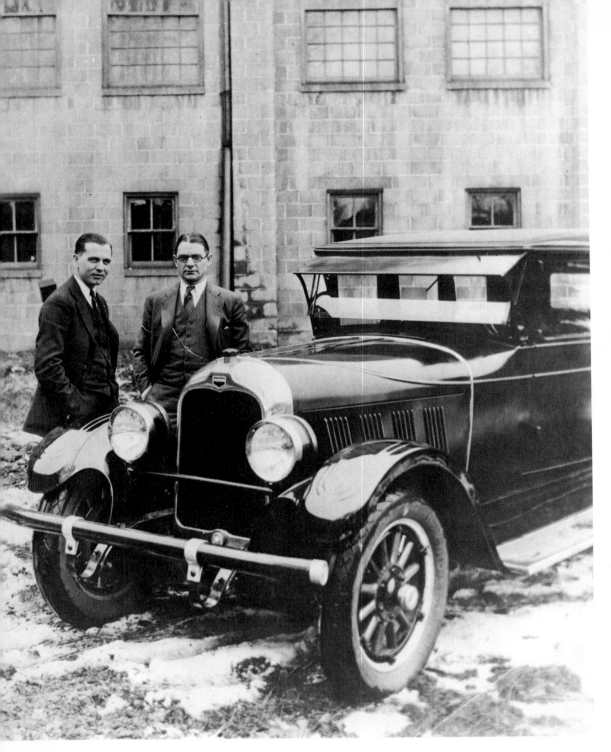

LEFT: E. L. Cord (left), who brought new life to the ailing Auburn company, with fellow-director Roy Faulkner and a 1928 Auburn (*Auburn-Cord-Duesenberg Museum*)

. . . And, too, because of the striking beauty of this car, which is proving day by day, in the possession of enthusiastic owners throughout the country, an outward indication of a new and wonderfully exhilarating motoring experience.

Childe Harold (he *hated* the name his Byron-loving parents had inflicted on him and always tried to be known as C. Harold Wills) had poured out his soul on the mechanical engineering of the Wills Sainte Claire, with its Hispano-inspired ohc V8 engine, but its pedestrian styling belied its internal merits. Perhaps Wills' ability to appreciate fine coachwork had been eroded by his long association with the Model T which, though black, was far from beautiful . . . Sales reached a peak at 1500 in 1923 and in 1925 the V8 engine was supplanted by an ohc six-cylinder. This lasted only one season before being replaced by a dull pushrod ohv unit, presumably as a cost-cutting exercise. Inevitably, the Wills Sainte Claire was just a memory by the end of 1927.

An even less successful venture into overhead camaraderie was the 1922 Leach, produced by a firm whose principal clientèle resided in Hollywood and for whose benefit the cars came equipped with the 'exclusive California top'. This was a sort of solid hood with ornate bevelled glass windows and side curtains to convert the car from 'an open to a sumptuous and weather proof Sedan type'. The Leach '999' had an ohc engine of almost Bugatti-like external cleanliness, reputedly designed by the famous racing car engineer Harry Armenius Miller, 'a thing apart from ordinary motors'.

'You must sit behind the wheel of this marvellous new car,' Leach instructed potential owners:

and touch the accelerator to sense the bigness and brute strength of this engine that is destined to become the standard by which all other motors shall be judged. From two miles per hour to seventy-five miles in high gear is a matter of seconds. Ten and three-tenths of 18 per cent grade has been negotiated in forty-one minutes, including turns and switchbacks . . . From the tip of the

ABOVE: Burlesque comedian Roscoe Yates and his Auburn 8-88 speedster, the sportiest of the new body styles introduced by Cord (*Auburn-Cord-Duesenberg Museum*)

ABOVE: Another attempt to market a luxury steamer, the 1924 Brooks was built in Canada as well as the US (*Harrah's, Reno, Nevada. Photo: Nicky Wright*)

LEFT: Murphy built the coupé body on this 1925 Doble Series E luxury steam car, Abner Doble's personal vehicle (*Harrah's, Reno, Nevada. Photo: Nicky Wright*)

radiator to the sheen of the patented nickel-plated rear collision bumper and luggage carrier, the Leach is the aristocrat of the highway.

Nevertheless even 'unusually complete equipment' (including a golf bag on two-seat models) failed to be sufficient inducement to persuade the public to go on buying Leach cars after 1923. The mid 1920s were difficult waters for the smaller independent manufacturers. In those sink-or-swim years of fierce competition for a larger share of a growing market, many independents took the only way open to them . . . and sank.

In 1922, for example, there were 181 American automobile manufacturers; by 1923 the number had shrunk to 108 and in 1927 there were only forty-four. The industry had moved in peaks and troughs. This is shown by the fact that the highest level ever had been 275 manufacturers in 1911 with precisely a hundred less in 1912. In 1919 there had been only ninety-five; in 1920 there were 132 and in 1921 there were 160. Some of the ephemeral models were obviously doomed to a mayfly existence by their sheer mechanical eccentricity. Examples of these include the Rotary Six, a $6000 touring car which probably went no further than the first prototype; the Kurtz, which boasted 'automatic gears' (actually a preselector mechanism); the Coats, and Gearless Steamers. There were others, however, like the Fox Air-Cooled Car which deserved a better fate than early extinction.

The Fox Air-Cooled Car was designed by Ansley H. Fox, a famous armament manufacturer, who made the guns used by President Theodore Roosevelt on his hunting expeditions. He used all the skills of gunsmithing on the cylinders of the Fox, which were cast separately with their cooling fins milled down to a uniform thickness and the cylinder heads fitted onto a tapered shoulder on the cylinders to avoid the need for gaskets.

'This amazing aircooled car,' claimed its maker:

hurdles a decade of motor progress . . . It cannot be gauged by existing standards because it transcends them . . . It cannot be compared to any other car because it is unique and unparalleled in the history of motordom . . . Never, at any price, has a more graceful and beautiful car been built . . . Every line of the low-hung body is in exquisite taste . . . A slight movement of the accelerator releases a surge of irresistible power. A further movement – the thrilling hum of fifty horsepower . . . In flexibility, acceleration, hill-climbing ability, power and versatility the Fox can be compared only to the most highly-developed types of water-cooled cars.

Sadly, the principal customers for the few Fox cars that reached the market seem to have been bootleggers who used that 'irresistible power' to outrun the Revenue men . . .

Dagmar was another marque which merited a better fate. It was built in Hagerstown, Maryland, from 1922, succeeding the Crawford car which was established in 1905. Crawford's interests were acquired by Mathias Peter Möller, who owned the Möller Pipe-Organ Works in Hagerstown. Möller had originally emigrated to America from Denmark so when he brought out a sporting 'Custombuilt' version of the Crawford he called it the Dagmar, in honour of Queen Dagmar, Princess of Bohemia and wife of King Valdemar the Victorious, who had ruled Denmark from 1202–41.

It was a handsome car, with straight 'military' wings, disc-covered artillery wheels and brass trim, and originally carried the arms of Denmark on its radiator (though this practice was discontinued after 1924 at the express request of the Danish Embassy). Several hundred Dagmars were built, using either Continental or Lycoming engines, both six-cylinder units.

The Dagmar was noted for its tasteful colour schemes, usually in subdued pastel colours, and also featured some of the most stylish bodywork of its day. Its premium model, the Sports Victoria, was used by Miss America 1925 to promote the charms of both herself and the marque. Soon afterwards, another Sports Victoria was bought by Daredevil Lockwood, the Human Fly, who climbed high buildings using sucker pads for grip. Unfortunately Lockwood came unstuck shortly after taking delivery of his Dagmar and plunged to his death from a high ledge on a skyscraper. Several hundred Dagmars had been built by the time 'the car you will like better at the journey's end' ceased production in 1927. The Pipe-Organ Works kept going, however, and was still in operation half a century later.

Even Peerless, one of the mighty 'Three Ps' (Packard, Peerless, Pierce-Arrow), was showing signs of senile decay in the mid 1920s. Richard H. Collins took over the management of Peerless in 1921. Collins, despite having had very little formal education, had succeeded Henry Leland as president of Cadillac. When Billy Durant, the erratic head of General Motors had been ousted, Collins soon followed him into the wilderness,

ABOVE: Wheel from the 1924 Brooks steamer (*Harrah's, Reno, Nevada. Photo: Nicky Wright*)

amid speculation that he was to become head of a subsidiary of Billy's new venture, Durant Motors.

Collins, in fact, formed a new company of which Durant was a stockholder. He then took it into Peerless with Durant under a curious agreement which sold the Collins Motor Car Company to Peerless for $500,000 and undertook to pay Collins a royalty of $65 per car as soon as the six-cylinder Collins had earned a million dollars. The Collins car never, however, passed the prototype stage and the stockholders of Peerless began asking questions. Though they gave Collins a vote of confidence, he had to repay Peerless $150,000, renounce his bonus and take a salary cut from $150,000 to $75,000.

Collins resigned two months later and was followed by four presidents in five years while the once unquestionable quality of Peerless engineering began to fade. Peerless had always built its own power units up to 1925. In that year a Continental Six was adopted and Peerless started to become just another quality assembled car with little externally to distinguish it from all the others.

Until the mid 1920s, the low-production quality marques had at least been able to offer more style than the mass-produced models. But, in 1926, Alfred P. Sloan, the former roller-bearing manufacturer who had risen to head General Motors, wrote to Harry Bassett, the general manager of Buick, suggesting that a styling division should be set up. As all the cars on

ABOVE: Detail from the 1922 Wills Ste Claire A-68 Roadster (*Briggs Cunningham Automotive Museum. Photo: Nicky Wright*)

73

LEFT: 1922 Wills Ste Claire A-68 Roadster, powered by an ohc V8 on Hispano-Suiza lines (*Briggs Cunningham Automotive Museum. Photo: Nicky Wright*)

ABOVE: 'Cadillac's cheaper sister' – the LaSalle. This example dates from 1933, the last year of the V8 (*Wirt Firman, Fort Wayne, Ind. Photo: Nicky Wright*)

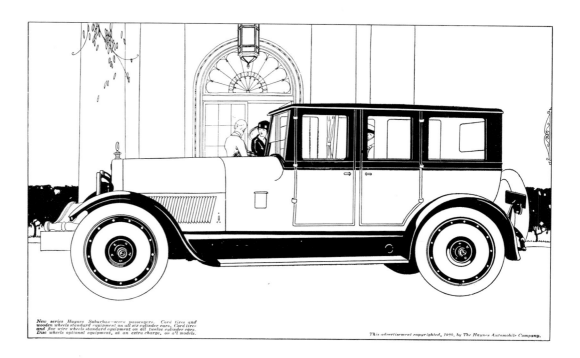

ABOVE: The Dagmar, claimed its maker, the Maryland pipe-organ maker M. P. Moller, was 'the car you will like better at the journey's end' (*Keith Marvin*)

the market were 'fairly good mechanically', theorized Sloan, appearance had become a dominating factor in sales, and therefore on the future prosperity of his group. The fundamental point, in his view, was whether GM was as advanced in terms of 'beauty of design, harmony of lines, attractiveness of colour schemes and general contour of the whole apparatus' as it could be. It was time that a car was designed as a whole, rather than as two disparate entities – namely the chassis and the body . . .

RIGHT: The Haynes Suburban (*Contemporary illus.*, Vogue, *1920*)

Sloan had already called in outside help on the recommendation of Lawrence P. Fisher, general manager of Cadillac. Fisher was one of the six brothers who had founded Fisher Brothers, the coachbuilding company that had been absorbed by General Motors in 1919 as its body division. Fisher had been visiting dealerships across America. One of these was Don Lee of Los Angeles, and Fisher was impressed by the designs being turned out there by Harley Earl. Earl was using the relatively new technique of designing bodies in modelling clay rather than hammering prototype forms out of metal over a wooden former. This enabled him to design a vehicle as a whole, blending body, wings, running boards and lamps into an aesthetically pleasing whole, as well as improving the proportions of a production model by lengthening the chassis.

Cadillac offered Earl a special contract to come to Detroit in 1926 to work with the Cadillac body engineers on a new marque they were developing as a lower-priced running mate for Cadillac. This was the LaSalle which, as conceived by Earl, looked remarkably like the French Hispano-Suiza. GM were so anxious to give this new 5-litre V8 a 'European look' that they paid Hibbard & Darrin a $25,000 consultancy fee, plus a monthly retainer of $1000 during the currency of the model, to use the 'Hibbard & Darrin hood and fender treatment' on the LaSalle. The era of the annual styling change – inducing a sense of dissatisfaction in the car-buying public with their 'old' model plus the wish to trade it in for the latest look – had arrived.

Many of the weaker marques were unable to meet the challenge of the mass-production stylists and quietly slipped into oblivion even before the depression began to take its toll. Often, few even noticed their passing. Alfred O. Dunk of Detroit was one of the few who did. As an appraiser in bankruptcy, he assisted in the obsequies of no less than 725 motor manufacturing concerns and recorded that, of 1301 distinct marques which had entered the industry during his business career, all but twenty-six had also made their exits.

Mr Dunk, however, had a conscience and, where there was no parent or affiliate company to gather up the pieces, took over whatever specifications and spare parts existed so that owners of orphan cars could keep them running a little longer. Once the demand for parts for a particular marque had ceased to show any financial return for Mr Dunk, he turned over the specifications – free of charge – to the National Automobile Chamber of Commerce on condition that they should make them freely available to anyone who needed them for an obsolete model. Single-handed, he had created a 'white elephants' graveyard' of the American motor industry.

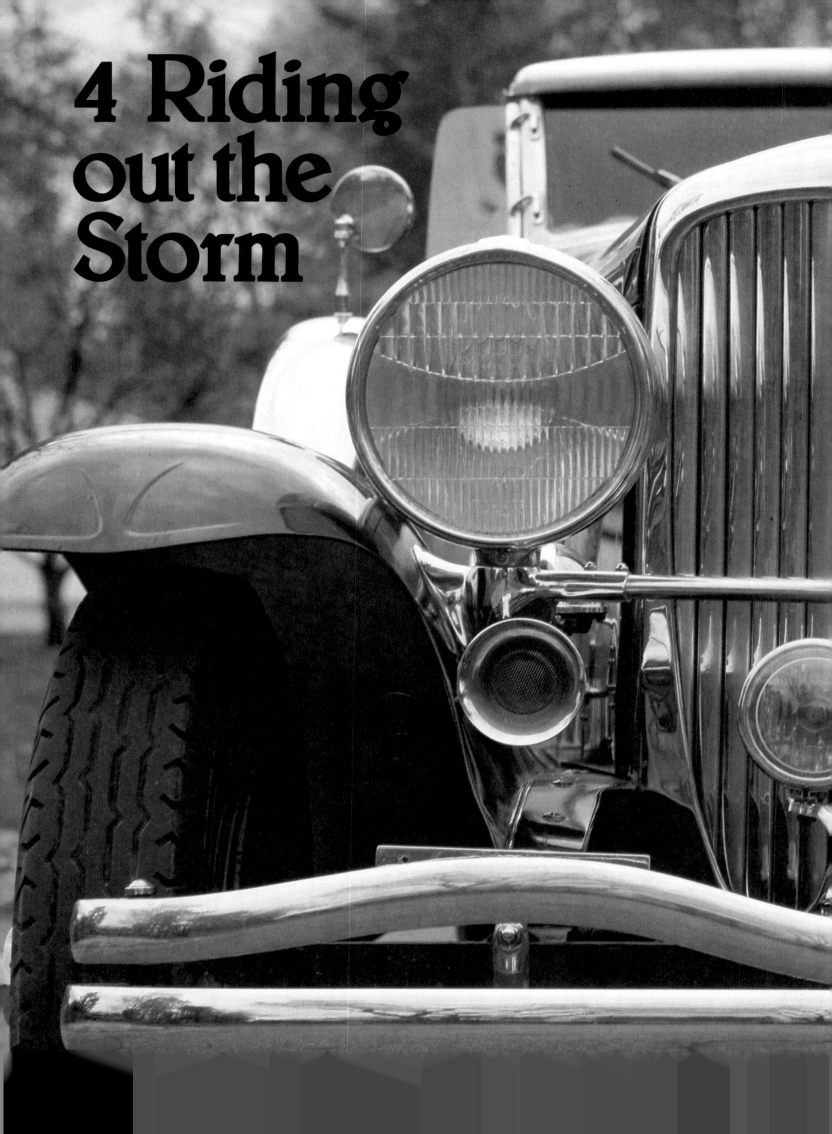

4 Riding out the Storm

With the Depression little more than a year away, the American motor industry seemed blissfully ignorant of the wrath that was yet to come, though the signs and portents were there in plenty. The events following 'Black Tuesday' in 1929 were really only the accentuated continuation of a trend that had been apparent for some time before. While the mass-producers had been vying with one another to produce better cars for less money, the smaller independents had been struggling to make enough money to build enough cars.

Those low-volume producers who were part of large groups could at least cushion themselves against falling sales on the success of the more popular lines; those who had no reserves to fall back on just put a brave face on things. Certainly there was no lack of confidence when the 1928 models appeared:

Oakland, Hudson, Velie, Essex, Willys-Knight, Hupmobile, Moon, Dodge and Paige, to quote but a few, have now bodies which are of the type admired in Europe, low-built with relatively high sides and the low but wide windows that give a touch of distinction to a car's lines . . . Many of the new cars are parti-coloured, and vividly so at that. Further, Chrysler and Reo show what are in fact allweather bodies, which, in conjunction with the new sports type Stutz, Duesenberg and Auburn, may indicate that the pendulum of thought is swinging back to open bodies again.

Moon's latest model is the 8-80 Aerotype – aeroplanes seem to be influencing cars in both Continents – with a French-designed body of only 70 in. overall height . . . Jordan shows an "Air-line Eight" – again the aeroplane – the new Packards have particularly vivid body colouring for the larger chassis, and Franklin have varied the more sombre shades by blue-grey with vermilion brake drums and wheel hubs. Stearns-Knight bodies are green with black moulding red-striped, and with the wheels green and red.

PAGES 78 AND 79: 1931 Model J Duesenberg with Murphy coupé body (*Auburn-Cord-Duesenberg Museum. Photo: Nicky Wright*)

RIGHT: A publicity photograph of a 1929 Auburn Phaeton in the giant redwood forest in California (*Auburn-Cord-Duesenberg Museum*)

TOP: Hupmobile New Century, 1929 (*Carl Price, Rolling Hills, Ca. Photo: Nicky Wright*)

ABOVE LEFT: Hupmobile New Century, engine (*Carl Price, Rolling Hills, Ca. Photo: Nicky Wright*)

ABOVE RIGHT: Hupmobile New Century, dashboard (*Carl Price, Rolling Hills, Ca. Photo: Nicky Wright*)

Possibly these more vivid colours will show through the mud coat the American car always carries at home; more probably it is due to an exhibition of what one could do with cellulose painting if one really tried, which took place recently.

The era of vivid colours had sprung from the fortuitous discovery in the DuPont research laboratories, on Independence Day 1920, of a chemical reaction which eventually led to the formulation of a nitrocellulose lacquer. This was given the trade name Duco. With this, a lacquer base could be created which would carry a higher proportion of suspended colour pigment than existing paints, thus allowing the use of brighter colours. Moreover, the new lacquer dried quickly, which was a great boon in mass-production terms for, previously, the only quick-drying finishes had been stove-enamelled funereal blacks.

Duco was, however, a troublesome infant. At first it had poor adhesive qualities and was prone to strip away from the metal panelling, while it relied on natural resins which were not available in vast quantities and were of variable quality. The latter problem was not resolved until the advent of synthetic resins. Three years of research in the General Motors and DuPont research laboratories ironed out most of the problems and, late in 1923, the first production car finished in Duco – the 'True Blue' Oakland – rolled from the production line. In 1925 Duco was made available to the entire car industry. Its adoption removed a major bottleneck from the production process for, in the days of coachpaint and varnish, it could take between two and four weeks to colour-finish a car. That could mean that a maker turning out 1000 cars a day needed covered accommodation for 18,000 cars that were in various stages of the paint process – an area of some twenty acres tied up unproductively. Duco cut finishing time to around one day, reduced the cost of colour finishes and greatly increased the range of colours available.

Purchasers of custom coachwork were soon able to specify even more exotic finishes. In November 1927 an iridescent varnish appeared which owed its shimmering appearance to a final coat of varnish incorporating thousands of fish-scales. Fleetwood used such a varnish on several 1928 custom bodies on Cadillac chassis. In 1928, according to legend, the same company accidentally introduced the first metallic paint.

Cadillac had commissioned Fleetwood to build three custom bodies to be finished in maroon and grey; but the job had to be completed in a shorter time than usual. Fleetwood therefore ordered the paint from DuPont and immediately painted the cars with the maroon. When the paint had dried, it was noticed that it was twinkling with tiny particles of metal and investigation proved that the ball-bearings used to crush the basic pigment had flaked under pressure, releasing metallic particles into the red japan pigment. Two of the bodies were stripped and repainted but there was insufficient time to repaint the third, which was put on exhibition just as it was – and attracted tremendous attention. It was not always easy, however, to repeat the fortunate circumstances that had led to the creation of that first metallic paint. Until 1932 metallic finishes were still scarce and expensive, even on custom coachwork. Even with the simple Duco, custom bodies were still subjected to the old sixteen-coat treatment, with the paint lovingly rubbed down between every hand-applied coat.

Sometimes colour was used in a truly extraordinary manner. On the 1929 Ruxton, for example, the stage designer Joseph Urban was employed to devise novel colour schemes and produced a design consisting of horizontal rainbow bands of colour. But then the Ruxton was no ordinary car. A component of a group known as New Era Motors Incorporated (which also included Moon, Gardner and Kissel), the Ruxton was definitely designed for those whose taste ran to 'something rich and strange' for it was said to be almost a foot lower than any other car of its day, thanks to the use of front-wheel drive.

The car had been conceived by Archie M. Andrews, a financier who was on the board of Hupmobile, and it was named after a friend of Andrews, William V. C. Ruxton, who was an enthusiast for front-wheel drive (and a possible source of extra finance). The Ruxton was powered by a 4.3 litre Continental straight-eight and sold for up to $5000. While the open versions, bodied by Raulang, the former electric car manufacturers, were strikingly handsome, the sedans were less distinguished (except for those adorned by Mr Urban), because their bodies were built by Budd using the same body dies as the British Wolseley.

Woodlite parabolic headlamps and a gearlever projecting from the dashboard were among the many unusual features of the Ruxton, though it was

ABOVE: 1927 Kissel Model 55 six-cylinder Coupé Roadster with pull-out 'mother-in-law' seat on the running board (*Harrah's, Reno, Nevada. Photo: Nicky Wright*)

perhaps fortunate that a plan to fit the curious Lever engine (designed by the Reverend Alvah Powell) into the Ruxton was stillborn. Twenty-five Ruxtons were built in the Kissel factory, and anything between twenty-seven and 475 more (production estimates vary greatly) were assembled in the Moon factory. By 1931 Moon, Ruxton and Gardner were all out of business though Kissel lingered on for a couple more years, dreaming of marketing a car based on the Lever-engined Ruxton – one of the wilder examples of *avant-garde* technology to emerge during the Depression. Before they became lost down such unprofitable side-tracks, Kissel had built some of the finest sporting cars of their day such as the 1929 White Eagle Speedsters, available with eights of 4 or 4.9 litres, plus internally expanding hydraulic brakes (and a golf-bag mounting on the rear mudguard).

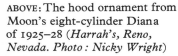

ABOVE: The hood ornament from Moon's eight-cylinder Diana of 1925–28 (*Harrah's, Reno, Nevada. Photo: Nicky Wright*)

ABOVE RIGHT: This elegant DuPont Model G Royal Town Car carries formal coachwork by Merrimac, and is capable of over 80 mph (DBW)

1929 was, in any case, an inauspicious year for bringing out any radically new model, as Erret Lobban Cord had found. He had been expanding his manufacturing empire, moving into aviation by acquiring the Corman Aircraft Corporation of Connersville, Indiana, and then, shortly afterwards, the Stinson Aircraft Corporation of Detroit. His various enterprises were combined under a central holding company, the Cord Corporation, which on 1 August 1929, could report assets of over $28.5 million.

The scene was set for the introduction of a new car line bearing Cord's name, and a worthy running-mate for the new super-luxury Duesenberg J, introduced a few months before. Cord had chosen to employ front-wheel drive for his new model, and had engaged one of the few American engineers with practical experience of this configuration to design the car for him. Carl Van Ranst had worked with Harry Armenius Miller on Miller's fast front-wheel drive racing cars which had dominated the Indianapolis 500 since 1926, and consequently the new Cord car followed the general layout of the Miller, with a De Dion-type front axle and inboard front brake drums. It was powered by a straight-eight Lycoming of 4934cc, similar to the unit used on the Auburn 120, but with the crankshaft extended at the forward end to take the flywheel. 'Docile and dignified in town, yet capable of unusual speed on the open road, the Cord commands your attention,' ran the publicity. 'The principles employed in its front-wheel-drive unit have withstood the rigorous test of racing, while its low, sweeping lines suggest amazing acceleration and power.'

Less endearing was a steering ratio requiring four turns lock-to-lock; the edge was taken off that 'amazing acceleration' by an all-up weight of over two tons and a gearbox and final drive assembly containing uniformly ill-chosen ratios, which cut top speed to a little over 80mph. But the Cord *was* outstandingly handsome; its overall height of only 61in and a wheelbase of 137in, plus a rakish vee grille, gave maximum opportunity to the coach-builders.

LEFT: Wheel and running board of the Model J Duesenberg (*Auburn-Cord-Duesenberg Museum. Photo: Nicky Wright*)

There were four standard models – sedan, brougham, cabriolet and phaeton – at prices from $3095 to $3295, while two town cars and some boattail speedsters were built to special order. Unfortunately the launch of the Cord L-29 at the 1929 Paris Salon was only days before fast-tumbling shares heralded the start of the Wall Street crash on 24 October and sales, though consistent, were small. Additionally, the car proved expensive to maintain as the timing chain was inaccessible, and the slightest front-end bump could cause expensive derangements of the driving and steering gear. Prices were slashed early in 1931 to $2395–$2595, but to no avail. Within a year production had ended after 4429 L-29s had been built.

BELOW: The final assembly line in the Cord plant, circa 1929, with L-29 sedans in production. Note the X-braced chassis frame (*Auburn-Cord-Duesenberg Museum. Photo: Nicky Wright*)

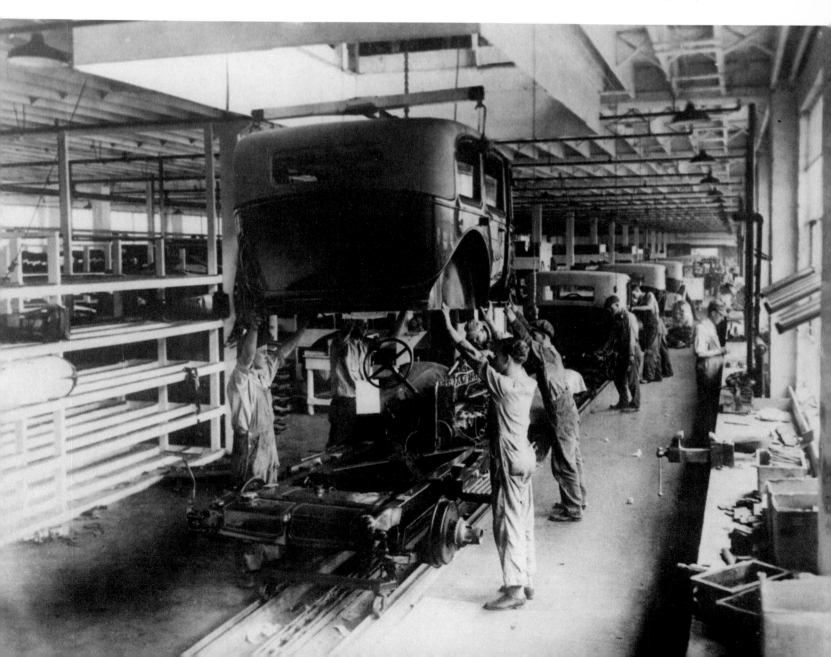

It is also likely that, even before the price cuts, the Cord was fairly massively underpriced; for the lean, low styling and radiator shell of the Cord were cribbed unashamedly by Walter Chrysler on his 1931–33 Imperial eight-cylinder line. This, available with semi-custom coachwork by LeBaron, cost just $3220 in two-seater roadster form. And Chrysler was selling these custom models at a loss to promote sales of his humbler products . . .

Chrysler ordered a total of 400 semi-custom bodies from LeBaron (out of a total Imperial production run of 3200 cars) and these were available right through the Imperial's production life. In 1934, incidentally, Briggs

ABOVE: 1931 Cord L-29 Cabriolet with Union City coachwork (*J. Coburn, A-C-D, Museum, Photo: Nicky Wright*)

ABOVE RIGHT: 1932 Chrysler Custom Imperial Model GL with Le Baron four-door convertible coachwork. BELOW RIGHT: 1933 model with Le Baron dual windshield phaeton body (*Frank Kleptz, Terre Haute, Ind. Photo: Nicky Wright*)

ABOVE: E. L. Cord (right) poses proudly with company officials alongside the new 1929 Cord L-29 sedan (*Auburn-Cord-Duesenberg Museum*)

absorbed the entire LeBaron organization, which became little more than a prestige nameplate on Briggs' bodies. Briggs itself was to be absorbed by Chrysler in 1952 when its British subsidiary was acquired by Ford. LeBaron's bodybuilding subsidiary, the Bridgeport Body Works, had been sold off by Briggs in 1930 as part of a retrenchment programme. It was reacquired by its original stockholders who decided to continue it as a 'specialty body business', whose staple product was to be station wagons, especially on Packard chassis.

The Chrysler LeBaron was one of the most practical of all the classic American automobiles for its elegance was not linked to excessive mechanical complication. Chrysler's engineering 'three Musketeers' – Fred M. Zeder, Owen R. Skelton and Carl Breer – had produced an engine which had a crankshaft running in nine main bearings, breathing through a dual-choke downdraught Stromberg carburettor, and driving through a four-speed gearbox with 'silent third'. In its original form the 6324cc power unit developed 125bhp, and was subsequently developed to give 135bhp, sufficient to move the Imperial of over two tons at speeds in excess of 80mph.

The Wall Street crash wrote 'finis' to the hopes of many of the smaller producers of quality cars, some of which offered true distinction (though

whether these distinctive features were always advantageous was a moot point). Typical of these casualties of the Depression was the Davis from Richmond, Indiana, which (along with its sister marque, the New York Six) offered the Parkmobile, a jacking device that raised the car on four legs and fitted with castoring wheels so that the car could be pushed sideways in and out of restricted parking spaces. Gardner of St. Louis built a prototype front-wheel drive chassis in 1930 as a successor to their 1926–29 straight-eight with four-wheel brakes and centralized door locking.

A similar design emanated from one of the most insubstantial of all American factories, which had existed under the name 'Hamlin-Holmes' from 1919–29, building approximately one front-wheel drive car each year with each vehicle differing in design from the next. Renamed plain 'Hamlin' for 1930, the company announced a final fwd prototype, suspiciously resembling the Gardner. It may not even have been completed. Cunningham, an anachronistic survivor from an earlier age, struggled on until 1931. It then ceased building cars to concentrate on its hearse and ambulance lines for which there was a continuing demand, as well as building bodies for proprietary chassis.

This was quite a popular activity during the Depression, as de luxe bodies on relatively humble chassis were deemed, by the remaining rich, to be preferred – for some special uses – to ostentatious exotica. The unemployed were likely to hurl brickbats at passing Cords, Duesenbergs, Packards *et al*.

One of the finest American makes to go under in the Depression was the DuPont, backed by the wealthy industrialist E. Paul DuPont, and produced at a leisurely rate appropriate to a carefully handmade luxury artefact. Just 537 DuPonts of all types were constructed between 1920 and 1932 and even at its peak production was only four cars a month. Best known of all the DuPont models was the Model G Speedster, with a 5278cc Continental straight-eight, bullnosed radiator grille and Woodlite parabolic headlamps, capable of a claimed 114mph.

Model G was also available in a suaver incarnation. Harrah's Automobile Collection in Reno, Nevada, preserve a delightful Model G 'Royal Town Car' in their vast collection of automobiles. With a flat-fronted radiator and quietly elegant coachwork by Merrimac, this car is the very antithesis of the stark speedster. Its original price was $5750 and it had a top speed in excess of 80mph. The discreet rear compartment, separated from the open chauffeur's seat by a wind-up dividing screen, has a formal English reserve in its upholstery and appointments and incorporates such features as an electric telephone for communicating with the chauffeur and silken roller-blinds to all windows.

The DuPont, though its character was different in many ways, was perhaps one of the few American cars that could be compared with the Rolls-Royce which, during the 1920s, was actually built in America to cut the costs of importing chassis from England. Rolls-Royce of America was set up in Springfield, Massachusetts, and around fifty British craftsmen were sent over to Springfield with their wives and families to set the operation in motion. Between 1921–29, Springfield was to build 2601 Rolls-Royces – both Silver Ghosts and New Phantoms. As production progressed, so the cars gained an increasing American accent, using more and more components from domestic sources, such as 6 volt electrics instead of 12 volt, left-hand steering and a three-speed gearbox instead of four. In October 1925 Rolls-Royce of America purchased the old-established coachbuilding company, Brewster of Long Island City, New York, with the idea of limiting Brewster coachwork exclusively to Rolls-Royce chassis which were fitted with a temporary box body and driven (one imagines in great discomfort) from Springfield to Long Island City.

When Rolls-Royce introduced the Phantom II in 1929, it was decided to stop production at Springfield due to lack of finance, though the factory had sufficient spares on hand to assemble a further 350 Phantom I chassis. These – even though they were totally obsolete – it contrived to sell from 1930–33, alongside a further 121 Phantom IIs with left-hand drive which were imported from England and fitted with Brewster coachwork. In 1934 Rolls-Royce of America Inc. was wound up, and the remnants formed into a new company, Springfield Manufacturing Co., headed by John S. Inskip, former head of Rolls-Royce of America. This firm marketed 'Brewster' cars, which were actually custom coachwork on Ford and other chassis, fitted with a distinctive heart-shaped radiator grille and flared wings. The situation turned full circle in 1937, when the Springfield Manufacturing Company was liquidated and Mr Inskip became the US importer for Rolls-Royce and Bentley, fitting some with custom coachwork bearing his own name.

The late 1920s also saw a disastrous shift in the fortunes of Pierce-Arrow, whose sales had begun to slip in the middle of the decade because of its policy of aiming at the uppercrust market only, without any 'cushioning' range in a lower price bracket. So a 'cheaper' Pierce-Arrow, Series 80, was launched, to be updated as Series 81 for 1928 by stylist James R. Way.

Unfortunately for Pierce-Arrow, the new look was almost the James R. Way to dusty death, for not only were the new models encumbered with a brash Art Deco look that alienated the conservative customers who bought Pierce-Arrows, but they also carried their name on the radiator. This was a *gaffe* as crude as having one's initials embroidered on one's breast pocket (Packard, indeed, carried self-effacement to the extent that customers had the option of plain hubcaps, which were normally the only exterior part of the car to carry the Packard name, and that was even in very small letters . . .). The sales graphs kept on falling and the frightened Pierce-Arrow shareholders, noting that in the prosperous year of 1927 their company had managed to record a deficit of $783,000, were only too happy to approve a takeover bid from Studebaker. This company had risen, under its president Albert R. Erskine, to become the third most successful American car manufacturer in terms of assets in the mid 1920s.

Studebaker paid $9,573,998 for Pierce-Arrow; but the deal did neither company much good. Though Pierce-Arrow relinquished none of its standards of quality, it suffered by association with Studebaker which was, during that time, experiencing some marketing problems with a low-priced six-cylinder range called the Erskine which sold badly on its home market, though it was relatively successful in Europe. Pierce customers did not like buying their cars from the 'dual distributorships' that were established under the new regime. Their cheaper atmosphere did not invite those used to buying only the best – and the service that went with it.

Pierce sales for 1929 were 8000 and the company did well to hold 7000 in 1930. The new 5998cc straight-eight of 1929 was an excellent car and helped to boost the marque's sales figures. Afterwards, however, sales tumbled, falling to 2692 in 1932. By this point Studebaker, only too anxious to rid itself of this 'unprofitable white elephant', sold Pierce-Arrow to a consortium of Buffalo businessmen for a million dollars. Studebaker's

ABOVE: This Springfield-built Rolls-Royce Phantom I has cabriolet coachwork by Brewster of New York (*Auburn-Cord-Duesenberg Museum. Photo: Nicky Wright*)

RIGHT: 1930 Pierce-Arrow A7 Passenger Touring featuring low gear for hill climbing (*Harold Kixmiller, Indianapolis, Ind. Photo: Nicky Wright*)

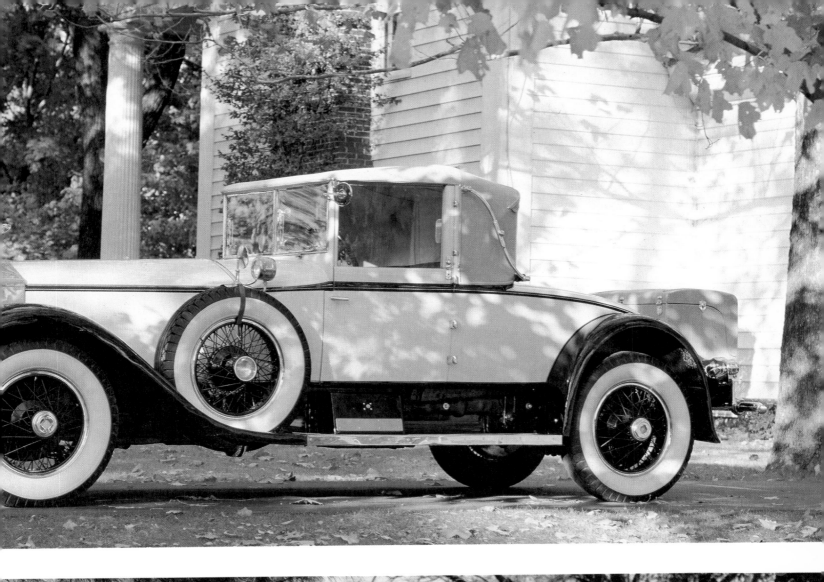

affairs were anyway in a parlous state thanks to the misplaced optimism of Albert Erskine. He was convinced that the Depression was only a state of mind, and that energetic marketing policies and exciting new models would bring forth hidden dollars from the consumers who had been hoarding them against such a show of confidence.

Erskine was proved wrong by the flood of apathy which greeted the Rockne, another low-priced model (named after a famous football coach who was killed in an air crash before the car was launched), and lost $2.8 million in paying out dividends to boost sales of Studebaker stock. In 1932 he paid $26,853,822 in Studebaker stock to take over the White truck company only to have the deal blocked by a consortium of White shareholders. Before this legal complication could be sorted out, Studebaker was placed in receivership with bank debts of $6 million. Three months later Albert Erskine shot himself in desperation. His company never fully recovered though astute management brought about Studebaker's discharge from receivership in 1935. Unfortunately the ills of Studebaker had mortally infected Pierce-Arrow; its new owners had spent a million dollars on a terminal invalid.

Another company which had had a stormy ride in the 1920s was Stutz, which had been taken over by steel tycoon Charles M. Schwab in 1922.

Schwab had obvious ambitions to extend his business empire firmly into the automotive field for, at an annual dinner of the National Automobile Chamber of Commerce, he pleaded for greater consolidation of the industry on the ground that only 'economies of scale' could make significant savings in production costs. He forecast that the existing sixty to seventy motor manufacturers would be cut to between five and ten (of which one, presumably, would be Stutz). But it proved difficult for Schwab to find the right calibre of executive for his new acquisition until, in 1925, Marmon reorganized its car manufacturing division, prior to splitting it away from their mill machinery division. Two men who left Marmon during this shakeup were to become president and vice-president of Stutz. They were Frederick E. Moskovics and Edgar S. Gorrell. Moskovics, a salesman with some engineering experience, had been vice-president of Franklin before joining Marmon while Gorrell, an ex-Army officer, had been one of the earliest military aviators.

Moskovics conceived a 'safety chassis' which appeared at the 1926 New York Show, powered by a 'vertical eight' 4.7 litre overhead camshaft engine designed by Charles 'Pop' Greuter, and with overall design by consulting engineer Paul Bastien, formerly with Metallurgique of Belgium. The Safety Stutz Vertical Eight was built exceptionally low because of a worm-drive rear axle, and used hydraulic brakes operated by a mixture of water and alcohol. A primitive form of safety glass was featured, with wire mesh embedded in windows and windscreen. Standard coachwork was designed by Brewster and was low and well-proportioned. Moskovics, who spent a good deal of time in Europe promoting the Stutz marque and keeping abreast of engineering developments (he was a close friend of Ettore Bugatti with whom he frequently exchanged notes on design developments) was the first American proponent of the Weymann fabric body. This was light and did not rattle, as well as making a major contribution to sound-proofing.

During 1927 the performance capabilities of the Stutz were amply demonstrated when Stutz cars were entered for all but one of the season's AAA races, and won them all. In the search for speed, Frank Lockhart, who developed the racing Stutz cars, conceived a boattail speedster with good aerodynamics. This was claimed as the first car of its type to go into production in America. At the end of that year LeBaron was engaged to redesign the range and, apart from bringing out much more elegant bodies, Ralph Roberts improved the lines of the chassis with continuous horizontal bonnet louvres, more graceful sweeps to the wings and larger headlamps.

In 1928 Lockhart attempted the Land Speed Record with a 3.1 litre Miller-engined super-streamlined 'Blackhawk' which, though it was to crash, showed itself capable of 225mph, which was faster than the aero-engine giants of up to eighty-eight litres used in other LSR attempts that year. A Stutz nearly beat the Bentleys at Le Mans in 1928 but sales were falling and, early in 1929, Moskovics was ousted. He was replaced by Gorrell. Edwin B. Jackson, who had been in the industry since 1902 and had worked at Packard, Willys-Overland, Wills Sainte Claire and Locomobile, became chairman and had the unenviable task of promoting sales of Stutz cars.

Against these failures and runs of ill-fortune, there were notable success stories. When custom bodybuilders were being forced out of business by falling demand, Enos Derham hit on the idea of converting a stock sedan into a town car. His brother James took the drawings of the conversion to a New York Packard agency and was successful in obtaining some commis-

ABOVE LEFT: The 1930 Pierce-Arrow mascot (*Harold Kixmiller, Indianapolis, Ind. Photo: Nicky Wright*)

BELOW LEFT: Building the 'World's finest car' – production line of the Model J Duesenberg in Indianapolis (*Auburn-Cord-Duesenberg Museum*)

sions. Such conversions, plus local repair jobs, kept Derham in business. In 1936 they proved that they could carry out a conversion on a stock Cadillac sedan cheaper than the Cadillac factory and were given the job of producing Cadillac's town cars as well. Among their clients at this period were Gary Cooper, Lily Pons (the Packard Town Car Enos Derham designed for this well-known opera star was his personal favourite out of all his designs), Harry Truman, King Farouk of Egypt, Pope Pius XII and Joseph Stalin.

Even more spectacular was the rise of Duesenberg during the Depression. Under Cord's management the Duesenberg brothers, Fred and August, had created the 'World's Finest Car' which they unveiled in December 1928 with unconcealed pride:

> *It is a monumental answer to wealthy America's insistent demand for the best that modern engineering and artistic ability can provide . . . Equally it is a tribute to the widely-recognised engineering genius of Fred S. Duesenberg, its designer, and to E. L. Cord, its sponsor, for these men in one imaginative stroke have snatched from the far future an automobile which is years ahead and therefore incomparably superior to any other car which may be bought today.*

The Duesenberg was big – the long wheelbase model was 12ft 9½in between hub centres, and the straight-eight engine displaced 6882cc – and costly, selling at \$8500 in chassis form. It was powerful as well, its engine developing a reputed 265bhp. This was more than twice the output of the

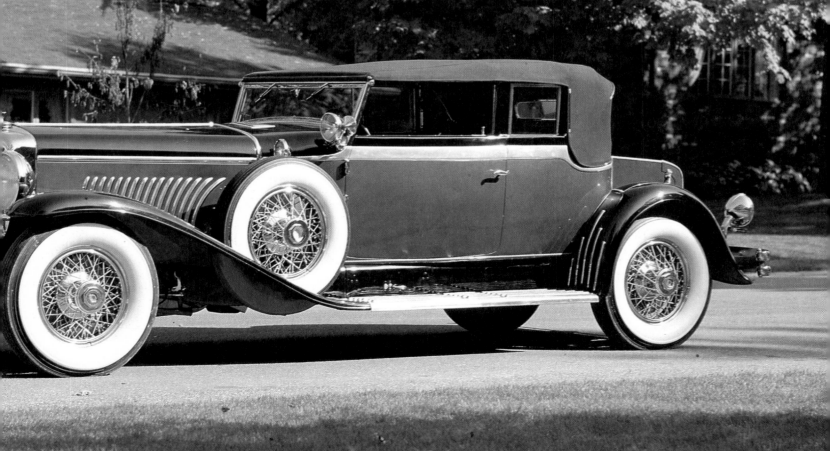

Chrysler Imperial, which (with 112bhp) had just claimed the title of 'America's most powerful car'.

In an era of low-stressed sidevalve engines, the Duesenberg unit was a remarkable *tour de force* of design for it was unashamedly derived from Fred Duesenberg's long experience of racing engines. It featured twin chain-driven overhead camshafts operating two inlet and two exhaust valves per cylinder, acting in hemispherical combustion chambers. The massive five-bearing crankshaft was balanced both statically and dynamically, and fitted with a torsional vibration damper consisting of copper-lined tubes bolted to opposite side of the crankshaft between the first and second throws. Pistons and connecting rods were of aluminium and the engine could run up to 4250rpm.

The Duesenberg chassis, with 8½in deep side members, was still massively heavy despite the extensive use of aluminium in the chassis and the number of forgings used, instead of castings, to save weight. Fitted with an open phaeton body, an average Duesenberg (if there was indeed such a thing) weighed over 2 tons 6cwt and a fully equipped limousine could weigh up to 3 tons. Hydraulic brakes all round seemed an essential part of the specification and acquired servo assistance from 1929 onwards.

In spite of its weight and the fact that it had only a three-speed gearbox, the Duesenberg was capable of 116mph and could accelerate from 10 to 80mph in twenty-two seconds. Instrumentation was comprehensive and included 150mph speedometer, altimeter, barometer, brake-pressure gauge, tachometer, ammeter, oil-pressure gauge, combined clock and chronograph and a set of four coloured lights worked by an ingenious device known as the 'timing box'. This incorporated twenty-four tiny sets of planetary gears,

driven from the fuel pump shaft. Every seventy-five miles the 'timing box' actuated a Bijur chassis lubrication pump which sent oil to all the chassis points. A red light glowed on the facia to show that it was working, while a green light came on when the Bijur reservoir was empty. Every 700 miles a third light glowed to remind the driver to have the engine oil changed and at intervals of 1400 miles the fourth light came on to tell him to have the battery water level checked at the next service station. Before being delivered to the coachbuilder each chassis was given a checkout of 500 miles on the Indianapolis Speedway. The Duesenberg was bodied by all the leading *carrossiers* of America and Europe: Bohman & Schwartz, Barker, Murphy, Derham, Hibbard & Darrin, Graber of Berne, Letourneur & Marchand, D'Ieteren Frères, Weymann and Gurney Nutting. The price of the complete car could be as much as $20,000, resulting in one convertible phaeton model being christened the 'Twenty Grand'.

The Duesenberg immediately found favour with the rich and famous. Among owners of the marque were King Alfonso XIII of Spain, Queen Marie of Yugoslavia and Prince Nicholas of Romania who had a 'Club Faux Cabriolet' by Letourneur & Marchand on one of his cars, and utilitarian sporting bodywork on the other – which he raced with great enthusiasm and very little success as shown by his three attempts at Le Mans in the annual twenty-four hour race. In 1933 he was disqualified, in 1933 his car seized up during the practice session, and in 1935 he retired during the race itself.

Fernandez & Darrin bodied a Duesenberg for film star Greta Garbo which cost $25,000; Garbo later sold this cabriolet to Suzy Vernon, a leading star of the French music halls. William Randolph Hearst, Clark Gable, Gary Cooper, Mae West, Elizabeth Arden, Joe E. Brown and Marion Davies were among other celebrities who owned Duesenbergs. The Model J may have been flamboyant and speedy but an even more spectacular Duesenberg was to appear at the very nadir of the Depression.

ABOVE LEFT: The Duesenberg Model J was certainly well-instrumented; lights on the 'timing box' even warned of oil and battery checks (*Auburn-Cord-Duesenberg Museum. Photo: Nicky Wright*)

ABOVE RIGHT: Detail (nameplate) from the Rollston-bodied Model J Duesenberg of 1934 (*Auburn-Cord-Duesenberg Museum. Photo: Nicky Wright*)

5 Selling the Sizzle

On a fine September evening in the early 1920s, the Overland Limited train was steaming across Wyoming into the sunset. At the window of the club car sat a man in his forties, idly watching the passing scene. Its bell clanging, the train slowed and halted at a wayside station. As it started again, a girl on a lean pony spurred forward to race the train as it gathered speed.

Though he now headed a motor manufacturing company, the man had not forgotten his early training as a journalist; something about the girl caught his attention and he realized that here was good copy for an advertisement. Snatching up a sheet of paper, he hurriedly began to write. His 'stream-of-consciousness' text was to become a classic of advertising, breaking away from the convention that car advertising had to be based on the mechanical advantages of the product, its horsepower, gearing and bodywork.

'Somewhere west of Laramie,' wrote the man, Edward S. Jordan, head of the company that bore his name:

There's a broncho-busting, steer-roping girl who knows what I'm talking about. She can tell what a sassy pony, that's a cross between greased lightning and the place where it hits, can do with eleven pounds of steel and action when he's going high, wide and handsome.
The truth is – the Playboy was built for her.
Built for the lass whose face is brown with the sun when the day is done of revel and romp and race.
She loves the cross of the wild and the tame.
There's a savor of links about that car – of laughter and lilt and light – a hint of old loves – and saddle and quirt.
It's a brawny thing – yet a graceful thing for the sweep o' the Avenue.
Step into the Playboy when the hour grows dull with things gone dead and stale.
Then start for the land of real living with the spirit of the lass who rides, lean and rangy, into the red horizon of a Wyoming twilight.

You might think that this was oblique gibberish, yet that advertisement has given Ned Jordan a kind of immortality. Which is more than it did for his product, for the truth is that the Jordan Playboy was really rather a dull car, much more of the 'tame' than the 'wild', and Jordan Cars were out of business by 1931. Nevertheless, Jordan was convinced that he had 'brought the rush and sweep of the open country . . . to the worker in the dull drab of the city office' with the 'swinging words of his copy' containing 'the reach of far-stretching plains, freedom, relaxation, moonlight on the open road, vagabonding in Arcady . . .'

Jordan was, anyway, the kind of man who believed in the romance of life; his biography was full – suspiciously so – of 'dramatic colour and adventure' and reads like a film scenario. The son of a woman who had piloted a wagon train west to Fremont, Nebraska, to open a general store, Jordan had grown up in the lumber camps of Wisconsin where he had found his first job at the age of nine, baling up wooden tiles for ten cents a day. Then he became a newspaper boy, and 'often in the gathering twilight the boy was to be found at the end of his route lying flat on his stomach on the warm ground, poring over the news from the great cities which he so longed to visit'.

Next, Jordan took a job in a plumber's shop next door to the local newspaper office, where he used to hang around after work.

'Deeply impressed with my interest,' recalled Jordan:

PAGES 98 AND 99: 'A cross of the wild and the tame', the 1926 eight-cylinder Jordan Playboy Model J roadster (*Harrah's, Reno, Nevada. Photo: Nicky Wright*)

OPPOSITE: The Case Complete '40' (*Contemporary illus.*, The Saturday Evening Post, *1913*)

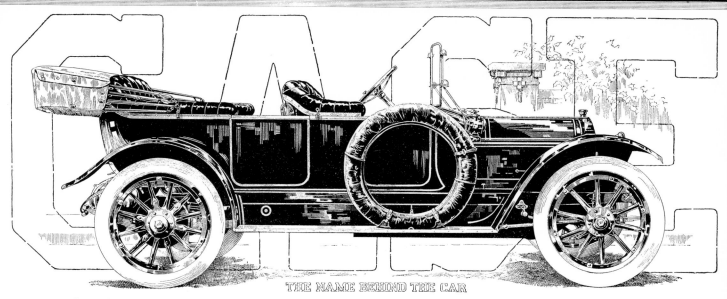

THE NAME BEHIND THE CAR

The Case Complete "40"

See What "Case Completeness" Means

Westinghouse Starting and Lighting Equipment.
Bosch Magneto (2-Point, Dual System).
Warner Autometer.
8-Day Clock.
2-Tone Electric Vibrator Horn.
Firestone Demountable Rims.
Extra Tire on Extra Rim.
Two Extra Inner Tubes.

Tire Cover.
Goodyear No-Rim-Cut Tires (37 x 4½).
Weed Tire Chains.
Timken Full-Floating Rear Axle.
Timken Front Axle.
Rayfield Carburetor, heated by both air and water, with Dash Adjustment.
Mayo Impulse Tire Pump.

Pantasote Top.
Electric Head Lights and Tail Light with Combination Oil and Electric Side Lights.
Work Light on Long Wire.
T-Head Motor (4½ x 5¼).
Forty Horsepower.
Wheel Base 124 inches.
Price, $2,300 (*including all the above equipment*).

We Are Able to Save Where Others Must Spend
Thus We Can Spend Where Others Must Save

A CAR may be completely equipped and be far from complete. For completeness as we mean it isn't confined merely to equipment.

The Case Complete "40" for 1914 carries every accessory that a motorist needs for touring.

It carries even an extra tire and tire cover on extra rim and two extra inner tubes. No other car that we know includes these in its price.

But the *vital* completeness runs throughout the *whole* car—to the parts that mean *long life*.

It lies in the materials and our methods of building—in our famous Hidden Values. Please judge by the following if you want them.

You Must Take Someone's Word

Trained *engineers* cannot judge steels on sight. They must test them in laboratories. Yet, if you want a car good for years of smooth running—

you must know that it contains them. And you must take someone's *word* for these values.

You can take our word for them in every Case Car. Please note the reasons why.

Whose Word You Are Taking

We've manufactured, for 70 years, the finest machinery the world can produce. Hundreds of thousands of customers know us.

They know we have maintained a standard throughout that no other maker has ever surpassed. We have a great reputation at stake—our customers' grandfathers bought of us. We make sure that nothing goes out that will lessen it.

These Costly Hidden Values in a $2300 "Forty"

These values are possible in a car at this price only for these reasons:

We are able to save where others must spend so we spend where

other makers must save. We had 9,000 dealers and 65 branch houses before we began making automobiles. Thus we saved an enormous selling expense. We saved on systems, on salaries, and on factory overhead.

We put all these savings into the car. All through these cars we effect a *completeness* that means strength and *permanent* smooth operation.

Get the Rest in Our Book

The Case catalog tells our story in full. Every man who wants a car should read it. It describes the Case Complete "40" at $2300, the Case Complete "35" at $1850 and the NEW Case Complete "25" at $1250. Three sizes, three horsepowers, three prices—all of Case Standard quality—all Case *Complete* Cars. See the Case "40," now ready for delivery. We shall appreciate your inquiry for our catalog.

Case Cars are sold through 79 branch houses and 9,000 dealers in the United States, Canada, South America and Europe.

J. I. CASE T. M. COMPANY, Inc.
500 Liberty Street, Racine, Wis.

The Case "40" is Now Ready for Immediate Delivery

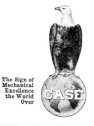

The Sign of Mechanical Excellence the World Over

CASE
The Car With the Famous Engine

The Sign of Mechanical Excellence the World Over

(181)

As a
Touring Car

Willys
KNIGHT

Touring Sedan
(Springfield Type)
Model 88-4

$1950

f.o.b Toledo

ABOVE: The Willys-Knight
Touring Sedan (*Contemporary
illus.*)

*the editor offered me a small job in the office and allowed me to run down
news and to write small items. So strongly did I feel this responsibility that I
almost wore the tyres off my bicycle in an effort to make good.*

Jordan, a precocious child, made a deal with the local telephone operator
who was in the habit of listening in to every conversation and passed on
any hot gossip for reprinting in the paper. 'So rapidly did the news
columns increase that in a short time, the paper was changed from a weekly
to a daily issue.'

Having discovered this journalistic talent, Ned Jordan used it to finance his way through the University of Wisconsin though he was spending so much of the time working for the *Wisconsin State Journal* when he should have been working for his exams that he had to rely on the 'royal good fellowship' of his friends to keep him liberally supplied with cribs. Eventually Jordan, aged twenty-three, armed with a whole crackerbarrel-full of homespun philosophy, became editor of the house journal of the National Cash Register Company but 'an interesting series of incidents,

BELOW: The Willys-Knight Touring Sedan (*Contemporary illus.*)

Willys KNIGHT

Touring Sedan
(Springfield Type)
Model 88-4

$1950
f.o.b Toledo

As a Sedan

dramatic but too interesting to relate separated young Jordan from his job'. When visiting his in-laws in Kenosha, Wisconsin, Ned met Charles T. Jeffery of the Jeffery motor car company and 'within two hours had been offered the position of advertising manager'.

He stayed with Jeffery for ten years, 'a continual stimulus to everyone around him' (one feels that Ned Jordan went through life in a flurry of advertising superlatives, selling himself with at least equal vigour as he employed on promoting motor cars) until he was offered backing worth $300,000 to prove that the car market had not reached saturation point.

His aim was to produce a car 'which was distinctly personal and which would build up goodwill' although, as the Jordan was to be entirely assembled from proprietary parts, it is difficult to see where that 'distinct personality' was to come from. At least it enabled Jordan to go quickly into production, for his factory was located in Cleveland where a group of bankers and investors had raised capital for his company, provided it was established in their town.

The marque grew, promoted by Jordan's purple prose, and was producing 10,000 cars a year after only eight years. Models like the Playboy and the Blue Boy followed Ned Jordan's dictum that 'The public wants a distinctive car, good looking, comfortable, and light of weight for economical operation: people get tired of living in houses that look just like everybody else's, and they feel the same way about cars.' Image was everything with the Jordan car which, like so many other marques, died in the Depression, confounding Ned Jordan's confident belief that: 'Almost any moment a good engineer, a good production man and a good salesman can get together and by bringing out a better looking, more comfortable, better performing, better serving car can take the business away from the big fellow even if he is firmly established . . .'

Well before General Motors came up with the concept of the annual model change, Jordan was already thinking along the same lines: 'In any business where there enters a style element there need be no fear of a monopoly. Just so long as women continually change their style of head dress and the length of their skirts, there is going to be a chance for every dressmaker. So it is with the car.'

Though Ned Jordan's freewheeling prose pointed automotive advertising in a new direction, it was already a well-developed industry. In 1919 automobile advertising had taken the lead, in terms of expenditure, in all media, and advertising was to hold this position throughout the 'classic' era despite the drop in sales during the depression. In 1914 a total of $1,438,000 had been spent on advertising in just one motor magazine, out of the industry's total expenditure of $4,115,000. By 1919 the industry was spending $14,750,000 in all media and in 1920 that single magazine (it was probably William Randolph Hearst's *MoToR*) took $3,709,000 in advertising revenue. That was almost exactly half of the total spent in product promotion in the American motoring magazines and, though the figure plummeted in the recession of 1921–22, it was back to $7,500,000 in 1923, rose to $8,750,000 in 1924, and was running at $11,000,000 by 1926.

That was purely the motoring media. In 1926 the leading fifty automobile manufacturers spent a colossal $41,000,000 between them to advertise their products in the national daily newspapers and the popular magazines. Publicity could also be a two-edged sword. As early as 1915 Cadillac copywriter Theodore F. McManus had written an advertisement entitled 'The Penalty of Leadership', which began: 'In every field of human endeavour, he that is first must perpetually live in the white light of publicity. Whether the leadership be vested in a man or in a manufactured product, emulation and envy are ever at work . . . When a man's work becomes a standard for the whole world, it also becomes a target for the shafts of the envious few.'

Though the 'Penalty of Leadership' spoke of the genius of Whistler, Wagner and the steamboat builder Robert Fulton, it did not mention the name of Cadillac anywhere in the four hundred or so closely set words of finely written prose. The car was exalted by implication, and the style of McManus's work so caught the imagination of the advertising industry that the advertisement was republished in 1929; the Cadillac company received over 100,000 requests for reprints of the advertisement. Moreover, when the magazine *Printer's Ink* ran a poll in 1945 to discover what had been the 'greatest advertisement of all time', the 'Penalty of Leadership' was voted the winner.

That spirit of 'emulation and envy' that it mentioned was certainly a potent force behind the collapse of what had seemed one of the brightest new stars to appear in the US repertoire of makes in the 1920s – the Rickenbacker, the 'Car worthy of the Name'.

The company's original advertising, which appeared at the start of 1922, explained the slogan: 'Probably no living man ever attained the singular distinction that properly falls to the lot of Captain E. V. Rickenbacker. Celebrated as one of our foremost automotive engineers – undoubtedly the dean of the world's race drivers and on top of that to come home from France as the American Ace of Aces surely places him in a position to have an experience with automotive mechanism and automotive requirements which no other man in the world could possibly possess. Associated with Capt. Rickenbacker in this enterprise are the industry's leading figures – Everitt, Flanders, Hood, Cunningham, Tichenor, Evans, Drumpelmann, Miller – all men who individually have held first line positions in the industry! Out of Capt. Rickenbacker's rare experience is born, what unbiased experts claim, is a new creation in automobiles.'

The Rickenbacker Six, which proudly bore on its radiator the 'hat-in-the-ring' emblem of Captain Eddie Rickenbacker's Escadrille Lafayette SPAD fighting scout aircraft, was backed by 'Barney' Everitt, whose Everitt Brothers body plant in Detroit was the second biggest in the world. Everitt, who had once been involved with the EMF car (irreverently known as the 'Every Morning Fix-it') called in the 'F' of that company to help him put the Rickenbacker on the market. This was Walter Flanders, a production expert who had made significant contributions to the rise of Ford. Notably smooth-running, the Rickenbacker Six was said to run from 2 to 60mph on top gear without the slightest trace of vibration as it had a flywheel at either end of the crankshaft. This, they claimed, was an idea that Captain Eddie had hit upon when examining the engine of a German aeroplane he had shot down.

The exciting news from Rickenbacker, however, came just over a year after the sales launch (and after four years of semi-secret development). This was the introduction of four-wheel brakes, the first use of this feature by an American medium-priced car, described by Captain Eddie as 'the greatest improvement in automobile engineering since the self-starter'. Packard had announced their adoption of this feature just sixteen days before Rickenbacker; soon after came three GM marques (Buick, Oakland, Cadillac) and some of the bespoke makers like Marmon and Locomobile, as well as more middle-class models like the Paige, the Chalmers and the Elgin. But those makers who weren't ready to fit front-wheel brakes to their cars (or couldn't afford the high costs of developing and putting into production such a feature) started a whispering campaign, claiming that the concept of four-wheel braking was unsound, and that cars so equipped were a safety hazard.

Studebaker, for instance, ran a nationwide campaign, taking full-page advertisements in the press to condemn four-wheel brakes; and though Rickenbacker issued advertisements and booklets to educate the American public in the advantages of brakes on all four wheels, Captain Eddie later went on record as saying that the whispering campaign was a potent factor in the failure of Rickenbacker in 1926, shortly after the introduction of the finest Rickenbacker of all, the stylish Super Sport, 'America's fastest stock car'. Powered by a twin-carburettor version of Rickenbacker's Vertical Eight engine, the Super Sport had lines reminiscent of some closed MGs, with a neatly streamlined 'torpedo' rear deck, cycle wings, and wire wheels. It was said to be capable of 95mph with four passengers and it carried a guarantee that it could do at least ninety.

A distinctive feature was the use of bumpers made from laminated mahogany, like an aircraft propellor, bound in brass and inlaid in a contrasting wood; bullet-shaped headlamps and safety glass all round contributed to the elegant appearance of one of the prettiest American cars of the middle 1920s. Even the persuasive pen of sales promotion director E. LeRoy Pelletier could not save the Rickenbacker. Pelletier, incidentally, was almost as colourful a character as Captain Eddie. *Motor World* called him a 'brilliant, plausible, rapid-fire conversationalist, a clever writer, resourceful far beyond the average . . . in the art of "putting them over," he has few peers'.

Pelletier had variously been advance agent for a circus, Klondike correspondent for the *New York Times*, telephone promoter, newspaper proprietor, real estate agent and car designer before joining Ford in 1905, where he devised the slogan 'Watch the Fords Go By' which, along with Packard's 'Ask the Man who owns One', was voted one of the two best-known auto slogans of all time. Having served with EMF, Pelletier (who claimed to have been 'the first man ever fired by Ford') joined Rickenbacker. 'Socially, it is good form to drive . . . Economically, it is good business', he wrote of the car which he was soon to promote in the immortal words:

To be seen in a Rickenbacker is to be classed with the cognoscenti and cultured', a phrase which attracted tremendous interest, some hostile, some adulatory, by its use of 'a new word in advertising copy'. Even that writer of the purple page, Ned Jordan, was moved to comment: *Of all the words I ever wrote, and I have written plenty, there's none that ever had the punch of this one . . . COGNOSCENTI . . .*

But Pelletier, who had said of the Vertical Eight Super-Fine that 'a Prince of the Purple might drive this car himself without losing caste', decided that it was time to get out when Captain Eddie handed in his resignation in September 1926, ahead of a 'vigorous reorganisation' of the company, and the marque's ultimate models, the 'European Type' 1927 range, died unsung, and the company went into receivership. A proposed 1924 merger with Peerless had failed to materialize . . .

During the 1920s a powerful new advertising medium – radio – had invaded the homes of America. As early as 1922, Henry Ford had operated

ABOVE: The 'new Fordor sedan' by Ford (*Contemporary illus.*, Ladies Home Journal, *1928*)

a company radio station in Detroit, though this was really more as an experiment than a means of promoting his products, and it was closed down in 1926. When launching updated Model Ts in January 1926 and 1927, Ford's 'old-fashioned orchestra' played almost-forgotten dances like the schottische, Virginia reel, gavotte, minuet and varsovienne (Ford's favourite), which had been popular when old Henry had been young. Many hundreds of Ford dealers set up loudspeakers in their showrooms and invited local people to dance to the music. In some places, a quarter of the populace crowded into the dealerships to dance to the Ford orchestra. But there was little publicity for the cars, and after that Ford turned away from wireless broadcasts for several years.

Others, however, moved in to fill the gap. In 1927, car manufacturers spent $133,506 in buying network time on the air. That year, there were 6.5 million radio sets in use in the United States, and the National Broadcasting Company put a second network into operation to meet the growing demand. Apart from Ford's 'Old Fashioned Barn Dance', listeners could tune to auto-sponsored programmes like Durant Motors' 'Heroes of the World'. In 1928 the Columbia Broadcasting System launched a third American network and Chrysler made an impressive scoop by sponsoring an interview with aviatrix Amelia Earhart immediately after her Atlantic flight – the first by a woman pilot.

Both Packard and General Motors offered more 'highbrow' entertainment. GM were first in this field with 'General Motors Family', a regular Sunday night programme which presented singers from New York's Metropolitan Orchestra, and which was broadened in scope in 1932 to include a symphony orchestra and guest singers and instrumentalists. By 1932 radio was big business: 55.7 per cent of American families owned a wireless set and car manufacturers spent a collective $1,863,436 on radio advertising, led by General Motors, whose annual budget was in the region of three-quarters of a million dollars, twice as much as the next biggest spender in this field, Hudson Motor Car Company.

Late in 1933, Ford came back on the air-waves, with Ford dealers paying a levy of $2 per vehicle sold to finance a nationwide musical variety show featuring the popular Fred Waring and his Pennsylvanians, the orchestra which had not only started the fashion for bell-bottom trousers in the Harold Lloyd film *The Freshman*, but whose members could muster such varied talents as 'crowing, hog-calling, whistling, imitating Katherine Hepburn, making queer faces or odd subhuman noises'. Ford also rivalled GM in sponsoring the Sunday Evening Hour, a programme of serious music played by the Detroit Symphony Orchestra, and featuring internationally-known stars like Yehudi Menuhin, and guest conductors including Sir Thomas Beecham. This was to become the most popular symphonic broadcast on American radio before it was suspended due to the war in 1942.

Car manufacturers sponsored an infinite variety of radio entertainment in the 1930s: Chevrolet backed the *G-Men* series, which presented dramatized versions of authentic criminal cases, while from 1936 to 1945 Chrysler sponsored *Major Bowes's Amateur Hour* at a weekly cost of $25,000. Bowes, they said at the time, 'sold Chrysler the way other people sell toothpaste'. Then Nash backed a cash question and answer game, *Professor Quiz*, while Hudson's speciality was *Hobby Lobby*, a programme featuring people with unusual and interesting pastimes.

'Radio,' remarked *Fortune* magazine sagely in the early 1930s, 'has almost ceased to be an advertising sensation. It has settled down to being an advertising success.' But it was noticeable that it was only the larger corporations that could afford to use radio as a publicity medium, just as it was these companies that had the size and flexibility to adjust to the changing patterns of demand in the ebbs and flows of the economic tide of the 1930s.

Ginger Rogers may have sung 'We're in the money' in *Gold Diggers of 1933*, but that year and the year after, the lack of finance due to the Depression meant that about 75 per cent of car sales were of the lower-priced models. As the situation improved later in the decade, demand for higher-priced cars grew again so that, in 1939–41, the low-price bracket only accounted for some 57 per cent of the market, about the same as in 1929.

'We responded accordingly,' recalled GM's patriarch, Alfred P. Sloan, who was all too aware that 'there have been and always will be many

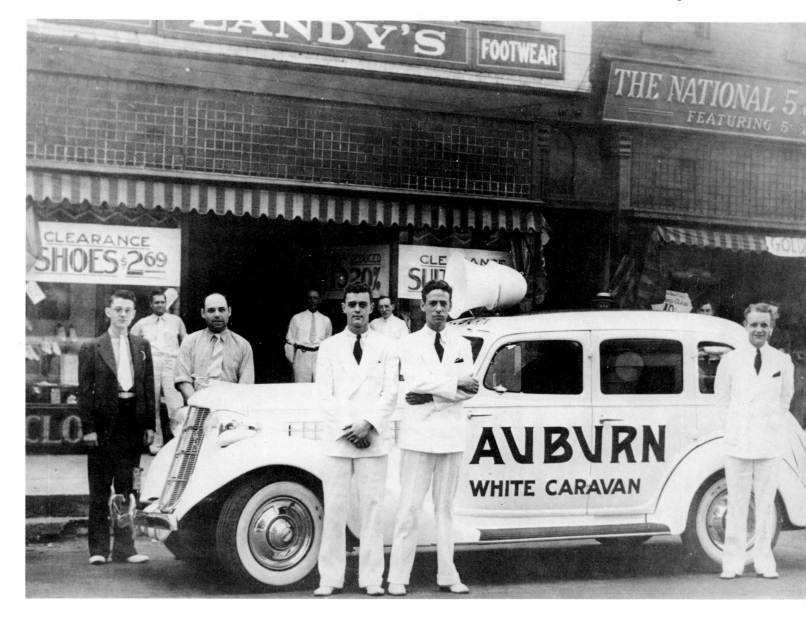

opportunities to fail in the automobile industry . . . the circumstances of the ever-changing market and ever-changing product are capable of breaking any business organisation if that organisation is unprepared for change.'

Gone were the days when simple imagery could sell expensive cars like the Duesenberg advertisements which, showing some rich nabob piloting his gigantic yacht or contemplating a cathedralesque pipe organ in his palatial home, simply said: 'He drives a Duesenberg'. The era of 'seat-of-the-pants' advertising, ushered in so recently by Ned Jordan, had passed. Selling motor cars had become a multi-million dollar profession for corporate man to follow.

ABOVE: An advertising campaign of 1935 – Auburn's 'White Caravan' of white-painted 1935 models toured local dealerships (*Auburn-Cord-Duesenberg Museum*)

6
The Greatest

Thrill in Motoring

Reading advertisements for American luxury cars which appeared at the height of the Depression, it is almost impossible to realize that they were written at the same time as New York office workers would walk in the middle of the street when they left their offices at night, so that they would not be hit by businessmen jumping off skyscrapers to commit suicide.

For example, the following *Analysis of a Lincoln Owner* was written in 1930. This was the year that the US market plunged to 3,362,820 vehicles against the 1929 peak of 5,337,087 units, and kept on plunging, reaching 1,331,860 units in 1932. The *Analysis* has a fine Bourbon ring of total ignorance of the turmoil outside the palace gates:

Financial: *Although it is by no means necessary to be a millionaire to be a Lincoln owner, it should be remembered that the Lincoln is not in the price class for the many. The ideal Lincoln owner is one to whom price is no object and yet who enjoys the Lincoln's unusual economies.*

Residence: *Distance from a great city is no handicap to a Lincoln owner as there is an endless chain of efficient Lincoln depots throughout the world. Live wherever you wish; have as many country homes as you want and own a Lincoln.*

Ideas about travel: *The Lincoln owner should not be a stay-at-home, but rather should consider the world his playground and his base of business operations. The Lincoln is designed and built to carry its owner far, swiftly and luxuriously.*

Personal Taste: *The ideal Lincoln owner has exceedingly high standards of taste. Such an owner gets the greatest enjoyment out of the faultless upholstery, fittings, furnishings and finishing of a Lincoln car. The owner who is hardest to please in this respect finds the most unending satisfaction in a Lincoln.*

Education: *An owner does not have to be an engineer to appreciate his Lincoln, although leading authorities throughout the world proclaim the Lincoln 'As fine a motor car as it is possible to produce'. The more an owner knows about fine materials, modern precision limits of building and uncompromising ideals of craftsmanship, the more he appreciates his Lincoln car.*

General: *To sum up, the ideal Lincoln owner is a man of substantial means, he lives wherever his choice of his interests decide, he enjoys the superb luxury of his car for travel, for sport, social and professional expeditions. He demands the most in the way of luxury, he knows how good things really can be and his Lincoln car continues to surprise and delight him.*

Outside there were six million unemployed, 'forgotten men' joining the lengthening soup queues; five thousand banks had failed; and a million used cars, the legacy of high-powered sales campaigns of the late 1920s, were clogging the sales lots of America. Yet the copywriter cocooned in the safe environment of N. W. Ayer & Son (the Lincoln agency) was still appealing to clients with a multiplicity of country residences. Between a quarter and a third of America's motor agents went out of business and 'the spirit of Darwin rode the economic storm' but the makers of prestige cars, competing for an ever smaller segment of a fast dwindling market, flouted economic sense and brought out yet more exotic automobiles.

They had little choice. They could not hope to compete as 75 per cent or more of the market was now occupied by the 'Big Three' (GM, Ford and Chrysler), nor did they want to demean their name and possibly alienate their remaining clientèle by producing cars of inferior quality. Many com-

PAGES 110 AND 111: Ernest Seaholm's masterpiece, the 1931 Cadillac V16, the world's first production 16 cylinder car (*Otis Chandler, Los Angeles. Photo: Nicky Wright*)

panies had had to pay off some of their workforce, and naturally the least skilled men had gone first; those remaining would have had to take a cut in salary. Builders of quality cars also probably had extensive stocks of materials which they would want to use up before investing at an inflated rate in new items, provided they actually had sufficient cash in hand to do so.

The equation, as they saw it, was simple: use the resources they had to produce a superlative car which would stand head and shoulders above other luxury vehicles and they could not fail to attract rich customers. Unfortunately, most of the luxury car producers applied the same formula virtually at the same time; the result was an unparalleled production of new luxury models which ended badly for almost everyone.

Cadillac, backed by the seemingly inexhaustible resources of General Motors, started the ball rolling at the January 1930 National Automobile Show by unveiling the world's first production V16 car. It was designed by their chief engineer, Ernest Seaholm, who had headed the company's engineering division since 1923, pioneering the introduction of such features as chromium-plating and synchromesh transmission in 1928. Seaholm's innovatory power unit displaced 7.4 litres, had hydraulically silenced overhead valves and developed a claimed 165bhp at 3400rpm. Its twin-cylinder blocks were at an angle of 45 degrees, each with its own updraught carburettor system. A new 148in wheelbase chassis and exclusive coachwork by Fleetwood were features of the V16, which sold at prices ranging from $5350 to $9500. This magnificent motor car – it was joined in August 1930 by a V12 derivative – was to be the flagship of a determined assault on Packard's leadership of the speciality car market.

GM had set its sights high; a Rolls-Royce had been bought and torn down to see how it was put together, and how it would stand up to a 'phenomenal test' at the General Motors proving ground. Lawrence Fisher had engaged a former Rolls-Royce engineer, Maurice Olley, who had done much work on suspension, to improve the riding qualities of Cadillac cars. Olley instigated some of the Rolls-Royce test methods, such as swinging a car from overhead pivots to measure its moment of inertia, and measuring the spring rates of the suspension when it was actually fitted in the car. A 'bump rig' – Detroit's first – was another idea borrowed from Rolls-Royce. This was a crude forebear of today's rolling road tests that enable dynamic tests of suspension and ride characteristics to be made on a static car.

This was to be followed, in 1932, by Cadillac's 'K' test vehicle, a complete limousine for seven passengers equipped with weights which could be moved about to change the moment of inertia and front and rear suspension deflection while the vehicle was in motion. In this way, the best possible ride could be found by comparing 'seat-of-the-pants' impressions during a test session, as no instrumentation then existed which would determine accurately the optimum ride characteristics. It was a field of research which was eventually to lead General Motors to adopt independent front suspension.

Packard responded to the Cadillac initiative in July 1930 with a dual plan, the first part of which was the development of a new medium-priced Packard which would compete with Buick and LaSalle. Alongside this, Jesse Vincent was given the task of developing a new 'Twin-Six' designed for the 1930s. Two configurations were considered, one on conventional lines, the other with front-wheel drive; sufficient budget was allocated to build one fwd prototype for evaluation purposes. Both the engineering and

ABOVE: 1931 Cadillac V16
(*Otis Chandler, Los Angeles.*
Photo: Nicky Wright)

styling departments were keen on the front-wheel drive layout; engineering was keen because of the improved handling characteristics which could be achieved, and styling because of the low overall height that could be attained. A novel chassis was conceived for the fwd prototype, with a bolt-on front section that could be removed for ready access to engine and transmission. The gearbox was mounted ahead of the engine, the gearshift linkage running down between the cylinder blocks.

Leading stylist Alexis de Sakhnoffsky was brought in to design a low, purposeful sedan body for the new car, which stood just 5ft 6in tall; however, having made the car look elegant, the styling staff made it look as unlike a Packard as possible by fitting a disguised radiator shell, without the distinctive Packard 'yoke'. It looked more like a German Horch; the reason for this was to prevent any 'leaks' about this totally new model from damaging the sales of existing models. The subterfuge was not really necessary for the innate conservatism of the Packard management, still

ABOVE: Originally built for Joan Crawford, this Cadillac V16 town car was one of three constructed (*Hillcrest Motor Co., Los Angeles, Ca. Photo: Nicky Wright*)

LEFT: Style-setter of the early 1930s – the 1933 Graham Model 65 six-cylinder sedan (*Cliff Shepler, Buena Vista, Ca. Photo: Nicky Wright*)

115

ABOVE: Interior of the
Cadillac V16 town car
(*Hillcrest Motor Co., Los
Angeles, Ca. Photo : Nicky
Wright*)

under the leadership of Alvan Macauley, resulted in the fwd project being halted on the grounds that such a technically advanced model would not be saleable. (It also promised to bring teething troubles which, as introduction of the new model was scheduled for the end of 1931, might unacceptably delay the development programme.) In fact, sticking to the conventional rear-drive layout hastened the development work, and within eleven months from the start of the new model programme, the twelve-cylinder car was ready for the market.

On 17 June 1931, the tickertape on the floor of the New York Stock Exchange, so often the harbinger of evil tidings in the preceding months, tapped out the exciting news – the Twin-Six was back! The styling and specification of the new model were radical. The radiator grille was vee'd and its shape echoed in the headlamp shells and glasses while the massive bumpers incorporated oil-damped harmonic stabilizers to iron out road shocks. A chromium-plated, 'aircraft-type' instrument panel incorporated an automatic clock and electrically-operated fuel gauge alongside a full array of conventional dials. On the radiator cap was perched a mascot inspired by the Packard family crest which depicted a 'pelican in her piety' and dated back to the Middle Ages, having been brought to America in 1638 by Samuel Packard aboard the ship *Diligent* from England.

The 7292cc engine had hydraulic valve lifters and its twin blocks were at the unusually wide angle of 67 degrees. Aluminium cylinder heads were standard, and the power unit developed 160bhp at 3200rpm. Each engine was initially run in for an hour by being turned over by an electric motor, then given a six-hour test under its own power; this was followed by a further hour-and-a-quarter under its own power on the dynamometer to ensure that its output was up to specification. Only then was the engine installed in the chassis and given a road test of 250 miles on the Packard Proving Grounds, during which it received its final tune-up. Then, assuming that everything was satisfactory, the car was awarded Packard's 'certificate of approval'.

When it was introduced, the Twin-Six was offered only with 'Individual Custom' coachwork by Dietrich, ranging from a sport phaeton at $6500, a coupé ($6600), convertible coupé ($6750), and convertible Victoria ($6850) to a convertible sedan ($6950). These were the last bodies bearing the Dietrich nameplate to be built under Ray Dietrich's personal supervision (though it appears that demand was so slow that Packard was still supplying them in 1934). In 1932 Ray Dietrich left the company he had founded and went to help the three Graham brothers develop a stylish new model, the Blue Streak, which pioneered the use of skirted wings and made exciting use of compound curvature in its bodywork. Its style-setting good looks were even an inspiration to toy manufacturers, for the model car makers Tootsietoys brought out a whole range of miniatures based on the Blue Streak. The Blue Streak's introduction, however, was marred by the death of Ray Graham in a drowning accident. And it never achieved the hoped-for sales. Ray Dietrich then joined Chrysler's styling department. In the 1950s he again set up under his own name as an industrial designer in Grand Rapids, Michigan, with Tom Hibbard as his sales manager.

In his seventies, Dietrich admitted that, in his own eyes, not all his custom bodies were classics: 'I often had to build personalized bodies that I didn't like myself – but the customer was always right!' And his customers had included Franklin Delano Roosevelt, Emperor Hirohito of Japan, film stars and Maharajas.

The new Twin-Six was not exactly a runaway success. During the currency of Packard's Ninth Series from 17 June 1931 to January 1933 (Packard eschewed such vulgarities as annual model changes, making improvements as and when they became appropriate), only 549 Twin-Sixes were sold, against 16,064 of the various eight-cylinder models. Of those eights, 6750 were Packard's new Light Eight, launched at the January 1932 Auto Show. The Light Eight was a misguided attempt to break into the low-priced market. Though it had the same power unit as Packard's Standard Eight and a vee-radiator like the more expensive models (though swept forward at the foot into a 'shovel nose'), the Light Eight sold for less than $2000 ($1750 for the Sedan, $1795 for the coupé, coupé roadster and coupé sedan). Yet it cost virtually as much as the Standard Eight – which was $690 more in price – to build, which meant that Packard made little or no profit on each car. Packard persisted with this unwanted loss-leader for a year while development proceeded on a new low-priced model, using engineers brought in from the mass-production companies under the leadership of George Christopher, who had been at Pontiac and Buick. Packard's luxury Eight Deluxe line sold 1655 units during the lifetime of the Ninth Series, with prices ranging from $4715 for the cheapest phaeton to $7250 for the dearest custom model, the Allweather Sport Landaulet. To boost the dismal sales of the Twin-Six, it was available from January 1932 with a range of bodies built by Packard from $3650 upwards. Even when it undercut the Eight Deluxe by so great a margin, the Twin-Six did not sell. The Tenth Series, which only ran from January to August 1933, fared a little better; the Depression had reached its peak in 1932 and sales gradually improved.

At the request of the marketing division, the model names were changed, so that the Standard Eight became simply 'Eight', the Eight Deluxe became 'Super Eight' and the Twin-Six became the 'Twelve'. The advertising agency was convinced that the old names were acting as a barrier to sales because they sounded old-fashioned. They may have been right; in under eight months 2980 Eights, 1300 Super Eights, and 520 Twelves were sold. Equally, it may just have been the substantial price cuts on the new models that accelerated sales – and it was the more expensive models that showed the greatest relative increase in sales.

The lower prices were all the more remarkable because the overall specification of the cars was improved. A new X-frame chassis was used and power-assisted brakes were also fitted with four stages of boost which could be selected by a switch in four positions on the instrument panel to suit driving conditions. But Packard, along with all the other makers of luxury motor cars, was now facing competition from a totally unexpected quarter: Henry Ford.

Ford's 'new beginning', Model A, had certainly been the most successful new car of all time on its introduction in 1928. A million cars had been produced in sixteen months but its meteoric progress had fizzled out in the

BELOW: The rare and beautiful Packard V12 Dietrich Convertible Victoria Model 1006 Custom (*A. F. Mittermier, Fort Wayne, Ind. Photo : Nicky Wright*)

face of fierce competition from Chevrolet which offered a six-cylinder model against the four-cylinder Model A. 'We're going from a four to an eight because the Chevrolet is going to a six,' Ford told his engineers in 1929. 'Now you try to get all the eight-cylinder engines that you can.'

The engineers therefore acquired nine eights of various makes for old Henry to inspect. His Lincoln purchase had naturally inclined him towards the V8 configuration (though in the mid 1920s he had experimented with eight-cylinder engines in an 'X' formation), but the V8s he was shown, with separately cast crankcase and cylinder blocks, were too complex for his ideals of mass production. Ford at once ordered work to begin on developing a V8 with crankcase and cylinders cast as a single unit. 'Everybody said it couldn't be done,' recalled one of his engineers, 'but Ford said it could.'

And it was . . . The first prototype was ready in May 1930, the second

BELOW: This 1934 Packard V12 seven-passenger touring is thought to have been a New York City parade car (*Ruth Dougherty, Indianapolis, Ind. Photo: Nicky Wright*)

ABOVE LEFT: The Packard
V12's hood ornament (*A. F.
Mittermier, Fort Wayne, Ind.
Photo: Nicky Wright*)

ABOVE RIGHT: Engine detail
from the Packard V12 (*A. F.
Mittermier, Fort Wayne, Ind.
Photo: Nicky Wright*)

six months later, followed by a rapid outpouring of twenty-five or thirty
experimental V8s, all aimed at reducing production costs. By 7 December
1931, Henry Ford was convinced that his goal had been reached: he held a
long discussion on the V8 project with Edsel, then cleared the decks to put
the new car into production. Though by now sixty-eight years old, Henry
Ford personally directed the changeover, 'here, there, everywhere, order-
ing, directing, changing', like a human dynamo. The factory had already
begun initial production of a new 'corking good four', the 'Improved
Model A' which was ready for introduction early in 1932. Ford peremp-
torily ordered work to cease on this engine, then grudgingly reinstated it as
a lower priced option to the V8.

It was the V8 that made all the running when it was launched on 31
March, despite the background of some ten million unemployed, Washington besieged by an army of jobless war veterans, farmers in revolt against
bank foreclosures on their property, and a Presidency whose immense
unpopularity was reflected in the nickname 'Hoovervilles' which was given
to the shantytowns which had sprung up on derelict land in almost every
city.

Ford saw a symbol in his V8 that would help assist national recovery –
'the new effort which the public is expecting' – but warned: 'In times like
these everyone has to take some risk . . . If American manufacturers do
their utmost to start the wheels of industry and the materials men begin
to raise prices, the whole effort may be throttled . . .' A Massachusetts
paper responded by calling Ford 'an American Moses leading his people
out of the Land of Depressed Bondage into a new economic Land of
Promise.'

Significantly, the V8 offered many of the features previously only available on high-priced, limited production models, at little more than the cost
of the old four-cylinder Model A. V8 prices ranged from $460 to $650,
and for that the customer got the 30hp V8, with its sports car performance,

a choice of fourteen different body styles (thirteen of them designed by LeBaron), all-steel bodywork insulated from the chassis by rubber pads, with the additional sound- and vibration-deadening rubber insulators in the spring shackles and shock absorber linkages (the shockers were double-acting Houdaille hydraulic dampers with thermostatic control), and a three-speed transmission with synchromesh on second and top gears.

It was a remarkable car, with a 75mph top speed (though this was about 10mph more than the capacity of the cable-operated four-wheel brakes) and the capability of accelerating to 60mph from a standstill in 16.8 seconds. It handled well in skilled hands for the steering was pleasantly high-geared, and the distinctive burble of the big 3622cc V8 had a sensuous quality that no mere four or six could ever hope to match. But inevitably its hasty development showed in a number of early problems like leaking piston rings, heavy oil consumption, cracked cylinder-heads and the reluctance of the engine to fire on all eight cylinders in damp weather. Moreover, the chassis designed for the four-cylinder engine had not been upgraded in any way for the eight, and was still a ladder-type chassis with only three cross-members. Ford had predicted that he would produce 1.5 million V8s in the first year but only 212,057 were built in 1932, so that the British factory at Dagenham, which at that time brought its V8s in from Ford of Canada, was only allocated 911 cars.

Henry Ford, who up to then had eschewed the annual model change beloved of GM, had the V8 completely re-engineered in the winter of 1932, with a double-drop X-braced frame, longer wheelbase, stronger rear axle and increased cooling capacity. Engine output was raised from 65 to 75bhp by using aluminium cylinder-heads with redesigned combustion chambers giving the new V8, Model 40, the ability to sustain a speed of 80mph.

Undoubtedly the most exciting feature of the new Model 40 was its styling, which owed a little to the Graham Blue Streak and a lot to a young Lincoln stylist named Eugene Turenne Gregorie. 'Bob' Gregorie was a yacht designer by training, and had joined Lincoln in 1931 at the age of twenty-three. He had rapidly come to Edsel Ford's notice and had been put in charge of styling the new 8hp baby Ford designed in 1931–32 to save Dagenham from financial disaster. Edsel had been so taken with the appearance of this car, the famous Model Y, that he asked Gregorie to enlarge the design for Model 40.

With a raked-back, heart-shaped grille, flowing lines and gently-skirted wings, the Model 40 broke away from the conservative lines of its predecessor; to many, it is the handsomest car that Ford ever built, especially in its two-seater roadster form. Hollywood loved its lines: Joan Crawford had a snappy roadster with oversize cowl lamps and other extras to emphasize the car's sporty appearance. Small wonder that Ford advertised Model 40 as 'The Car without a Price Class'.

Model 40 put Ford back in the black in 1934, after the company had experienced three profitless years and in 1935 Edsel Ford promoted 'Bob' Gregorie to head of the styling department. They called it Edsel's haven for there he could be free from the 'pressures of corporate pragmatism'. In a dark corner of the studio he would pull the dust sheet from a discarded prototype and sit with his 'kindred spirit' Gregorie and talk of racing yachts.

The Ford V8 was not the only sensation to come from the Ford empire in 1932 for in that year Lincoln introduced its new KB, with a V12 engine. 'The workmanship beneath the bonnet is reminiscent of the best European practice, than which there can be no higher praise,' commented *The*

ABOVE: Powered by a 6.3 V8 engine, the 'low-slung and rakish' Lincoln Sport Phaeton dates from 1931 (*Promotions, Inc., Detroit. Photo : Nicky Wright*)

OPPOSITE: This Walker-bodied Franklin Six has full-elliptic springs all round (*Val Danneskold, Granada Hills, Cal. Photo : Nicky Wright*)

Autocar. But though the KB was 'one of those exceptional cars which in both construction and performance rise much above the general practice of contemporaries,' sales were disappointing. In 1933 only 2112 examples of the KB and its smaller mate, the KA, were sold. In 1934 a new Model K was introduced to replace both lines, with a 6784cc engine which fell almost midway between the capacities of the KA and KB. Sales rose slightly to 2170 for the year. Model K survived until 1940, though only 120 were sold in its last two seasons, including the famous 'Sunshine Special' for President Franklin D. Roosevelt.

Lincoln were the first makers of luxury cars to investigate aerodynamics. Henry Ford had been forced to suspend production of the famous Ford Trimotor aircraft – 'the Tin Goose' – because of the Depression, but the Ford wind tunnel was used to investigate airflow over the new KB bodies. As a result, they were notably free from excrescences though their styling was still conservative enough not to alienate the customers.

ABOVE: This handsome cabriolet version of the Ford Model 18 V8 was a limited production model from Ford of Germany (DBW)

RIGHT: Ford's V8 was advertised as 'The greatest thrill in motoring'. This is filmstar Joan Crawford with her 1934 V8-40 roadster (DBW)

The larger firms producing what were to become known as 'classic' cars were not alone in the curious belief that the depth of the Depression was an ideal time to launch V12s and V16s on the American market. Pierce-Arrow, still shackled to Studebaker, came out with two V12s in 1932, one of 6522cc, one of 7050cc. They did nothing to help declining sales which fell to 2692 for the entire Pierce-Arrow range in 1932, against 8000 in 1929 and 7000 in 1930. Like all Pierce-Arrows, the V12 was powerful and superbly engineered; Ab Jenkins, the Mormon Meteor, drove a 7571cc V12 prototype at an average speed of 112.9mph for twenty-four consecutive hours on the Bonneville Salt Flats to set up an unofficial American record. In 1933, he averaged 117mph for twenty-four hours – this time officially – in a stock V12 roadster, breaking fourteen international and sixty-five national records; his ultimate twenty-four-hour average, with a modified V12, was 127.2mph.

Franklin, which had remained steadfastly true to air-cooling since 1902, had abandoned some of its more eccentric design features in the intervening years. The laminated ash frame which had been used on all cars until 1927 was replaced by steel frames on long wheelbase models which then gradually ousted the older construction; but full-elliptic springs were a feature of all Franklins until 1932. From 1925, however, Franklin styling had been anything but eccentric, with leading designers retained to create elegant custom coachwork. The J. Frank de Causse-styled Series 11 of 1925 had led to an increase in orders, and de Causse had been followed by Ray Dietrich, whose 1929–32 Speedster was a styling milestone for the company. It was produced alongside such other memorable custom bodies as the Transformable Town Car and Deauville Sedan, both distinguished by little opera lamps mounted on the rear quarters, the Pursuit and the Pirate Touring.

In 1932, with sales running at only 1975 units for the year, Franklin's wantonly uneconomical marketing policies had brought the company to the verge of bankruptcy (in 1931, when only 2851 Franklins were sold, customers had a choice of *twenty-six* different standard bodies apart from the option of custom coachwork). Since 1928, the company had been planning a V12 with the aid of US Army aeroengineer Glenn Shoemaker; now, when the time was inauspicious, they decided to launch it. But in the effort to save money on the car, all the traditional Franklin features were discarded at the request of the banker's representative Edwin T. McEwen ('The Undertaker'). The chassis was a conventional pressed steel unit, riding on normal semi-elliptic springs all round. Proprietary axles replaced the Franklin units – tubular front, rear with light alloy differential – of the earlier models, and the bodies were apparently out of LeBaron courtesy of Lincoln, who had rejected them.

A proposal that the power unit should be an 8.9 litre giant was rejected, and a more modest displacement of 6.6 litres chosen. At almost three tons, the V12 was a ton overweight, yet nevertheless could reportedly reach 95mph; there was a mild attempt at forced induction, with the cooling air ducted to the carburettor under the control of the driver.

The Franklin V12 was offered at $4400, but found few takers (although the famous aviator Amelia Earhart was one of them), so for 1933 prices were slashed by 35 per cent. Even then, total sales of the V12 only reached 200. An attempt to build a low-priced model, the Olympic, was equally ill-fated. The Olympic was only a Franklin as far as the power unit and grille were concerned, the rest being a Reo, for economy. The public was not impressed and the closure of Franklin early in 1934 was a foregone conclusion.

Even less explicable was the policy adopted by Marmon to meet the Depression. From 1929–31, the company had offered a straight-eight at less than $1000 under the Roosevelt name. Then, at the January 1931 New York Motor Show, Marmon unveiled what the press called 'a car of exceptional interest' – a sixteen-cylinder that excelled even Cadillac's offering. The motoring press reported:

The V-type engine develops 200bhp and weighs only 4–5lb per horsepower. Aluminium alloys are used for the crankcase, cylinder blocks, heads, valve covers and many chassis parts; the pistons work in case-hardened steel sleeves which are pressed into the cylinder blocks. Overhead valves are operated by pushrods from a single camshaft placed between the banks of cylinders. The complete car weighs 2 tons 4½ cwt and the engine capacity is about 8 litres.

ABOVE: Marmon's 8046cc V16 was one of the great American classics. This is a 1933 Convertible Coupé (J. Dougherty, Indianapolis, Ind. Photo: Nicky Wright)

OPPOSITE, TOP: Boattail Speedster on the 1931 Auburn 8-89-A equipped with woodlite parabolic lamps (R. Kughn, Auburn-Cord-Duesenberg Museum. Photo: Nicky Wright)

OPPOSITE, BOTTOM: 1932 Auburn 12-161A Phaeton Sedan, bodied by central, with a 6412cc V12 engine (John Fleck, Auburn-Cord-Duesenberg Museum. Photo: Nicky Wright)

The saloon model has a striking appearance set off by a handsome V-fronted radiator with an invisible filler cap. The price is to be about $5000. The specification includes a hypoid-bevel final drive (ratio 3.7 :1), three forward speed gearbox, Bendix-Perrot brakes and Stromberg downdraught carburettor.

Styled by Walter Dorwin Teague, the 8046cc Marmon V16 was one of the great American classics; developing an alleged 200bhp, it nevertheless failed to find sufficient buyers. An eight-cylinder derivative was offered in 1932, but in 1933, the V16 was the sole Marmon on offer. An even more exciting and radical model, a V12, was, however, under development. Designer George A. Freers took two cylinders from the centre of each bank of the V16 to create the 6033cc V12 which was completed in April 1933. It had all-round independent suspension, coil and pillar at the front, four transverse leaf springs at the rear, and an $8\frac{1}{2}$in-diameter backbone frame which split into a 'Y' shape at the front, with the engine carried between

the forks of the 'Y'. The power unit weighed 850lb, against the 950lb of the
V16, and developed 151.5bhp at 3700rpm.

Styling, again, was by Walter Dorwin Teague who this time broke away
from tradition: the idea, apparently, was 'to overcome sales resistance to an
expensive car by radical new ideas.' Teague created a low roofline, and a
long bonnet line, which continued right back to the windscreen without a
scuttle, its length accentuated by horizontal louvres. The pontoon wings
were unlike anything that had been seen on a luxury car, and the headlamps
were faired into the front wings.

The car's performance was as exciting as its appearance: on test at
Indianapolis, it reached a speed of 95mph. But no orders were forthcoming,
and the prototype was the only V12 Marmon to be built. Though the
Marmon Car Company went out of business in 1933, the Marmon family
remained in the automobile industry, building Marmon-Herrington all-
wheel-drive trucks.

Only one other US manufacturer attempted to market a V16 car: Peerless.
Their 1930 range, styled by Alexis de Sakhnoffsky, consisted of three sixes
and an eight priced from $995 to $2195, which failed to sell despite their
sleek good looks and competitive pricing. Peerless therefore decided to
move the other way, and go firmly upmarket with a V16. The prototype
was a dramatic vehicle, making extensive use of aluminium alloy in its
construction, even in its chassis frame, which weighed a mere 42lb. Its
7.6 litre engine was said to produce 173bhp at 3300rpm, and the custom
coachwork was by Murphy.

It remained a prototype, and the last Peerless left the production line
on 30 June 1931. The plant remained idle for two years, until the 'Great
Experiment' of prohibition ended. Then Peerless decided to go into the
brewing business, and on 30 June 1934, changed its name to the Peerless
Corporation, brewers of Carlings Ale, a far cry from the clothes wringers

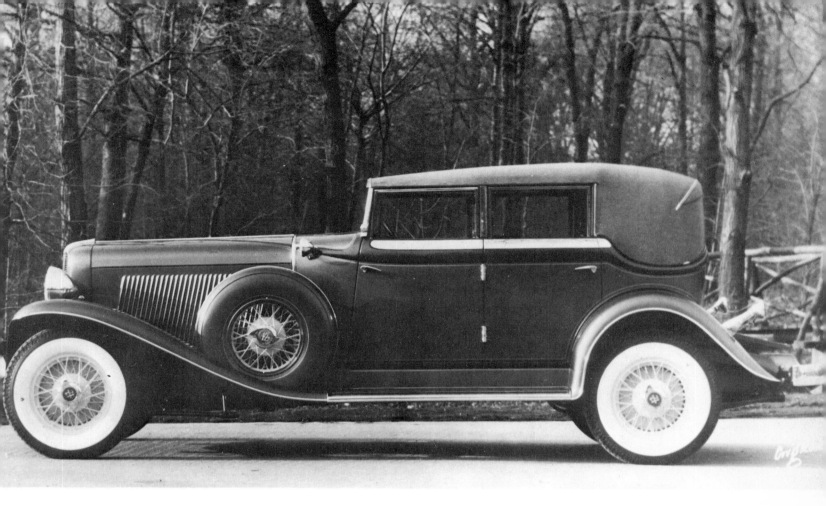

which had been the company's first product in Cincinnati in 1869.

Another company which acted out of character in an effort to defeat the Depression was Auburn. Their first move had seemed wholly sensible: faced with slipping sales in 1930, with only 14,000 cars finding owners against 22,000 the year before, Auburn had scrapped its entire range and replaced it with a new medium-sized eight in a short-term, one-model policy. The new car, the 8-98, had a Lycoming engine developed from the 1927 Type GU, but bored out to 4402cc, and developing 98bhp at 3400rpm; it was mounted in a rigid chassis with X-bracing, which was apparently the first time such a frame had been used on a rear-wheel-driven car.

Among the unusual features of the new Auburn were an LGS Free Wheeling unit (which could be actuated at will by the driver) and a Bijur automatic chassis lubrication system. At $995 for the sedan, it had proved so popular that Auburn sales for the year hit an all-time record of 28,000. For 1932 the eight was redesignated '8-100' with only modest design changes; alongside it, Cord introduced a kind of 'cut-price classic', a V12 which sold for less than $1000 in basic form, perhaps in an attempt to reach those whose fortunes had been diminished in the Depression.

Auburn designer George Kublin apparently drew on Lycoming's aviation expertise in designing the power unit which they were to manufacture for him (the fact that the Auburn-Cord-Duesenberg group had both automobile and aviation interests proved useful in keeping product technology up to the minute). With a swept volume of 6412cc, the Auburn V12 unit had its blocks set at an angle of 45 degrees, with a single camshaft set between them. This operated the horizontal valves through rockers; each valve had its own individual water jacket which could be removed to give access to the valves without disturbing the cylinder-head. The engine developed 160bhp, giving top speed of 100mph in standard trim. Performance was enhanced by a dual-ratio Columbia rear axle, product of yet

ABOVE: The 1933 Auburn V12 Phaeton Sedan sold for $1850; its 6412cc engine developed a healthy 160bhp (*Auburn-Cord-Duesenberg Museum*)

another A-C-D group member. 'High' (3.04:1) or 'Low' (4.55:1) ratios were selected on a dashboard switch which opened a valve linked to the inlet manifold, the vacuum in which was used to shift the ratios, giving a choice of six forward speeds.

The most desirable of the V12s was the Custom Speedster, a delight-fully-styled, boattail, two-seater with a devastating turn of speed. In 1932–33, this model captured the American Stock Car Speed Champion-ships with an array of speed and endurance records that encompassed speeds up to 117mph and distances up to 2000 kilometres. At only $1495, the Custom Speedster was sound value for money as well as one of America's most attractive cars; but the customers failed to materialize for either the V12 or the 8-100 and Auburn sales for 1933 went down to 6000.

Stutz, the other famous manufacturer of speedsters and stylish sedans, rather than follow the trend of adding more cylinders, brought out instead the ultimate expression of its well-proven, straight-eight power unit, the DV 32. They revived the old 'Bearcat' name for its speedster version, which was sold with a guaranteed maximum speed of 100mph (there was a short wheel-base speedster too, the Super Bearcat).

ABOVE: Dashboard of the SSJ Duesenberg (*Briggs Cunningham Automotive Museum. Photo: Nicky Wright*)

The DV 32 had four valves per cylinder, actuated by twin overhead camshafts, and developed 155bhp, no mean output from 5276cc. The crankshaft ran in nine main bearings, and a dual-choke Schebler carburettor was fitted. The Stutz DV 32, with a four-speed gearbox with close-ratio 'silent third' and the retention of underslung worm final drive to keep overall height to a minimum, had very little in common with contemporary American engineering practice, which favoured 'woolly' sidevalve engines and three-speed gearboxes. It was perhaps the very finest of all the luxury cars of the Depression, combining superlative engineering with elegant styling; typical of the detail refinement which set the Stutz apart from most of its contemporaries was the use of Lockheed hydraulic braking with variable servo-assistance controlled by the driver. The DV 32 seems even more remarkable when you consider that the only comparable American car, the Model J Duesenberg, cost $9500 in chassis form against $4995 for a complete five-passenger DV 32 Sedan.

In 1932, Duesenberg celebrated the Depression by launching an even more exotic version of the J, a supercharged model known as the SJ. It had a centrifugal supercharger, a device more favoured in America than in Europe, which revolved at five times crankshaft speed, delivering a 5lb/in boost at 4000rpm, and increasing engine output to a claimed 320bhp at 4750rpm (at which the blower was spinning at a frightening 23,750rpm!). Though its all-up weight was 46cwt, the SJ roadster could accelerate from 0–100mph in seventeen seconds. The factory advertised that the standard SJ four-passenger phaeton could reach a maximum of 129mph in top and 104mph in second.

The SJ was very similar to the J externally, though the bulk of the supercharger installation meant that an external exhaust system had to be fitted, which added visual glamour to the car. Mechanically, little was done to cope with the extra performance; the engine had larger crankshaft bearings, tubular steel conrods and stronger valve springs, and stronger front springs, equipped with Watson Stabilators, were fitted. Even the external exhaust system was not an infallible identification of the SJ, for status conscious Model J owners had the option of having the chromed external exhaust system fitted to their car at extra cost.

Most SJs were built on the same 142½in wheel-base as the short wheel-base J but two SSJ roadsters were built on an extra short 125in wheel-base chassis, and fitted with two-seat bodies made by another Auburn-Cord-Duesenberg subsidiary, the Central Manufacturing Company. Another distinctive feature of the two SSJs was the use of a 3:1 final drive ratio, against the standard 3.78:1 gearing. One SSJ was sold to Gary Cooper, the other to Clark Gable.

Total production of SJs is believed to have been about thirty-six cars, out of 480 or so Model J chassis built. Sadly, the SJ was to claim the life of its designer, Fred Duesenberg, who was killed driving an early SJ in July 1932. His brother August took over as chief engineer of Duesenberg, and it was under his aegis that the Mormon Meteor, Ab Jenkins, driving a specially-bodied SJ, averaged 135.47mph for twenty-four hours and 152.15mph for one hour on the Bonneville Salt Flats at Utah, establishing new international records that beat, by over 17mph, the previous figure for the hour achieved by Hans Villiez von Stuck in a racing Auto-Union at the Berliner-AVUS track. As a result of Jenkins' success, all subsequent SJs were fitted with a twin-carburettor supercharger device similar to that used on the record car which had a designed top speed of 200mph on the 3:1 axle ratio.

The Duesenberg SJ was a remarkable car by any standards.

CALIFORNIA
HISTORICAL
VEHICLE 36

Sheltering Palms

America's first automobile exhibition was held at the turn of the century but such was the interest in special coachwork that the first Automobile Salon was held on the top floor of Macy's in New York as early as 1904. By the 1920s these Automobile Salons, had become, very definitely, the showcase for the most superlative coachwork and, unlike the annual auto shows, were only open to the chosen few, with admission by invitation only. Among the draped flags and potted palms could be seen the finest chassis and most exclusive bodywork available on the American market; exhibits were strictly limited to American custom body builders and to imported chassis and coachwork. The Automobile Salons were really a kind of 'catalogue in the round' for the exhibitors were hoping to secure orders for replicas of the vehicles on display, modified developments of the exhibits, or single customs inspired by the general trend of the cars on show.

Four Automobile Salons were held each year, taking the exhibits right into the haunts of the wealthy. Undoubtedly the premier Automobile Salon was the one which inaugurated each season of shows, and it was held in the lobby of the Hotel Commodore in New York which had installed a limousine-size lift just for the annual Salon. In January, the Chicago Automobile Salon took place in New York's Drake Hotel, and then in February Automobile Salons were held in the Biltmore in Los Angeles and the Palace Hotel in San Francisco. Because of the widely spread venues for the Automobile Salons, manufacturers usually took no chances, but produced three or four examples of a particular body style, one for each Salon, which were then shipped to their destination by rail.

No expense or effort was spared to create an atmosphere of exclusiveness at these Salons; after the Ford takeover, Lincoln was an enthusiastic participant in such events (though Ford itself eschewed participation in motor shows, preferring to set up all-Ford exhibitions). Lincoln set up 'shows-within-shows', which it often referred to as 'the Lincoln Petit Salon'. Guests at such events, issued with engraved invitation cards, were greeted by 'doormen and other attendants appropriately uniformed and carefully schooled in the proprieties,' who escorted them to the Lincoln display. Here 'charmingly costumed' pages and salesmen in tuxedos, sporting white carnations, were ready to minister to the guests as they wandered round the Lincoln exhibit, 'a picture of exquisite appointments,

PAGES 134 AND 135: The 1933 Pierce Silver Arrow V12 (*J. F. Brucker, Los Angeles, Ca. Photo: Nicky Wright*)

BELOW: A typical exhibit at a 1920s motor show – the Auburn exhibit at the 1929 Montreal Motor Show, held 19–26 January that year (*Auburn-Cord-Duesenberg Museum*)

floral decorations, and perfumed fountains, further enhanced through artistic lighting effects.' Outside the hotel, drivers in livery were in attendance to demonstrate 'chauffeur-driven equipages' to prospective purchasers. Like the guests, the exhibitors were present at the Automobile Salons by invitation only, selected by the Salon's Board of Directors, and had to pay $500 for every car they showed. They were then allotted engraved invitation cards to send to prospective clients.

The Automobile Salons ran for a week at each location, following a pre-determined ritual, with every day reserved for a different set of guests. One day, for example, was reserved for suppliers of paint, trim, upholstery, leather and coach fittings; another was for the car manufacturers and their engineers. Rather like clothing manufacturers attending a couturier's fashion show, these men were at the Automobile Salon to glean ideas which could be translated into volume production terms and to determine the dominant styles for the coming season; this was where the designers of custom bodies could pick up fat consultancy fees. Chauffeurs had their own afternoon, for these paid drivers could often influence their masters in the purchase of cars and accessories, and would expect a handsome commission from the vendor for so doing. High society – the 'Four Hundred' – had its own afternoon and evening, carefully segregated from the period allotted to the *nouveaux riches* such as film stars, rich industrialists and those who had made their fortunes in trades which placed them lower in society.

What sort of vehicles were shown at the Automobile Salons? At the Salon in the Hotel Commodore in December 1921, for instance, the emphasis seems to have been on formal town cars. On the diamond-patterned floor of the Commodore and identified by discreet banners fastened to the wall, could be seen such vehicles as 'a handsomely finished Daniels Landau-Brougham, upholstery old rose of French cloth, woodwork mahogany inlaid with maple, the hardware and fittings specially made for this particular car' or the 'new Biddle with Rauch-Lang body, collapsible Town-Brougham upholstered in green, exterior black.' Against one of the entrance doors was a 'Fleetwood town car body on a Duesenberg straight-eight chassis, finished in dark blue with grey corduroy cloth interior,' while in other sections of the salon could be seen 'Brooks-Ostruk body on Minerva chassis, made for Billie Burke . . . the interior is in morocco goat-skin . . . the seats are fitted with air cushions which automatically adjust themselves to the passenger weight' or, from the same *carrossier*, 'town car on McFarlan chassis, price $11,650, exterior in two shades of French grey, interior grey broadcloth' or 'limousine on Minerva chassis, inlaid work by Driguet of Paris.' One of the most handsome bodies on show that year was a magnificent Healy limousine on a Stevens-Duryea chassis, with four individual seats like club armchairs and inset panelling with electric lights to enhance the club-like atmosphere, the exterior of this severely formal body being painted bottle green, picked out with contrast pin-striping.

The Automobile Salons continued to be the arbiters of fashion throughout the 1920s. It was at the 1927 Automobile Salon that 'opalescent' paint with a base of fish scales was first shown in public, while the accidental introduction of metallic paint caused a minor sensation at the 1928 Salon, which represented the high point of the series. The economy was still buoyant and there was an unusually large attendance for the New York Salon in December. Many fine European cars were on display, but it was remarked that the American luxury cars were now fully the equal of the imports. It was at this Salon that the Model J Duesenberg made its début.

RIGHT: An outstanding model
from Moon was the 1929
White Prince of Windsor
straight-eight (*J. R. Edwards,
Fort Wayne, Indiana. Photo:
Nicky Wright*)

BELOW: 1930 Cord 129
Brougham, bodied by Central,
a subsidiary of the A-C-D
group (*L. Starkweather,
Auburn-Cord-Duesenberg
Museum. Photo: Nicky
Wright*)

RIGHT: This poster was used to advertise the Ford Rotunda at the 1933–34 Chicago Century of Progress Exposition (DBW)

That year, the most popular body style was the convertible sedan, reflecting the increasing tendency of the wealthy to take the wheel of their own car, rather than employing a chauffeur. This had also encouraged luxury car-makers to improve the performance and road-holding of their products; a paid driver might not complain of any shortcomings in his machine, but a rich owner-driver was bound to do so.

The undoubted leader of style that year was Dietrich, whose convertible sedans were shown on several American and European chassis, notably (at the New York Commodore) on a Lincoln, which had a blue body, black wings and wheels and pin-striping in red and (at the Chicago Drake Hotel) on a Packard with a partridge cream body, pheasant green wings and chassis, and green wheels and striping. The motoring press noted that as far as the use of colour went, Packard was the undoubted leader, narrowly ahead of Cadillac. At the Salons, Packard distributed a catalogue of seventeen available custom bodies, while Cadillac had twelve.

RIGHT: Fashion was set from the top in the mid 1920s; Buick's 1926 Prince Sports Tourer cribbed unashamedly from Packard (DBW)

ABOVE: Shipping a Cord L-29 for exhibition overseas: the model made its European debut at the Paris Salon in 1929 (*Auburn-Cord-Duesenberg Museum*)

The 1929 Salons were minus some of the best-known names in the custom coachwork business. They had been stricken by the shortage of cash in July and August of that year when they were seeking finance for the next year's models, only to face cost-cutting programmes from several of their best clients, like Pierce-Arrow and Franklin. Holbrook was one of the first custom coachbuilders to go under at that time. Only Packard, it seemed, was able to weather the crisis, for it had started its own custom coachworks in 1928 offering its own lines alongside bodies by LeBaron and Rollston. Contrary to the popular trend towards closed cars, Packard's best-selling lines were open roadsters and phaetons, symbols perhaps of a last desperate fling before disaster struck. Nor did Packard have any low priced model available in 1929, having discontinued the six-cylinder range.

The last of the New York Custom Salons was held in December 1930, also heralding the end of the Chicago, San Francisco and Los Angeles Salons. The day of the independent custom coachbuilder was almost over.

United and Phillips had followed Holbrook into oblivion while Fleetwood was no more than a subsidiary of General Motors, serving Cadillac and LaSalle.

Dietrich, soon to be absorbed by the Murray Body Company, its majority shareholders, showed three Packard convertible sedans in 1930, one powder blue with red striping, cream wheels and appliqué basketwork trim, another finished in metallic maroon with tan wings. Rollston, a New York company owned by Julius Veghso, Sam Blotkin and Harry Lonschein, exhibited a number of town cars, plus a Packard convertible Victoria finished in metallic tan with matching upholstery, while Derham, with several cars on show, had a sport sedan as its star exhibit. LeBaron's magnificent contribution to this swansong of the custom era was a convertible sedan, again on a Packard chassis with the entire upper part of the body chromium plated in brilliant finish to the lustrous black of the remainder. Chrome wheeldiscs were also fitted. The interior was upholstered in pigskin, and twin spare wheels were carried at the rear. After the Salons, this car became the property of Mrs Walter Briggs, wife of the head of Briggs Motor Bodies.

Bereft of a suitable showcase for their talents in custom bodies, the quality car manufacturers jumped at the opportunity of displaying their models at the first of the great fairs of the 1930s, the Chicago Century of Progress Exposition, which opened in 1933. Cadillac built a 'fastback' sedan on the V16 chassis, a striking vehicle with horizontal bonnet louvres, pontoon wings and a lean, low look; a limited edition of duplicates was subsequently turned out by Fleetwood. This car was one of the star exhibits, helping to attract 10,200,000 visitors to the General Motors stand (of whom only 3000 bought new cars).

In the Travel and Transportation Building crowds queued for up to two hours to see Packard's exhibit, 'the Car of the Dome'. Reputedly the most costly Packard ever built, this twelve-cylinder Sport Sedan was designed by Ray Dietrich, built by Dietrich, Inc, and cost $12,000. Compared with the Cadillac, 'the Car of the Dome' was conservative in appearance. It was finished in golden bronze metallic paint with chrome wire wheels, and all the interior brightwork – even the accelerator pedal – was gold-plated. All the wood trim, as well as the interior bar, was in burled Carpathian elm and the bar opened to reveal four golden goblets, two flasks and a mirror with gold corner clips. There was also a fitted ladies' dressing case and the upholstery was in beige English broadcloth. In the rear of the car was a sheared beaver rug. The Packard, however, carried off every automotive prize at the Exposition.

In many ways the Chicago Exposition was an exercise in frivolity. Apart from the automotive exhibits, it featured national exhibits from all over the world, such as a Tudor village from England, and regional buildings from France and Germany; and it also featured entertainment booths, of varying merit, perhaps the most embarrassing of which was a display by a trio of whistling ventriloquists.

Though all the prizes went to the Packard, Pierce-Arrow's special car for the Chicago Exposition was the outstanding exhibit for many people. To modern eyes it is certainly the more stunning of the two. An interval of almost half a century has not lessened its ability to draw the crowds, which it still does today at the Harrah Museum in Reno, Nevada.

The Pierce-Arrow 'Silver Arrow' was described as the 'car built in the 1930s for the 1940s', and nothing like it had ever reached production status

ABOVE: The rare Speedster Runabout Packard Model 7-34 Seventh Series Eight, built in 1930 (*Harrah's, Reno, Nevada. Photo: Nicky Wright*)

in America. The Silver Arrow had grown out of a meeting in October 1932 between Roy Faulkner, Vice-President of Pierce-Arrow, and a stylist friend, Philip Wright, who had conceived an automobile with a totally new appearance. The first prototype was built in three months on a Pierce-Arrow twelve-cylinder chassis. In all, there were to be five prototypes and five 'production' Silver Arrows, each carrying a $10,000 price tag.

In many ways the Silver Arrow *did* forecast pretty closely the shape of luxury cars in the 1940s; its raked-back, 'snow-plough' radiator grille blended modernity with tradition in just the right measure. The headlamps were faired into the front wings, which were continued back on a rising line to flow into the belt line of a full-width passenger compartment with a tapering tail. The spare wheels were concealed inside the front wings; the pontoon-shaped rear wings were spatted to conceal the upper part of the wheel, and the only 'dating' feature of the styling was the tiny rear 'eyebrow' window which broke the smooth curve of the tail. Inside, the Silver

ABOVE: 'The car built in the 1930s for the 1940s, the 1933 Pierce Silver Arrow V12 (*J. F. Brucker, Los Angeles. Photo: Nicky Wright*)

LEFT: 1933 Pierce Silver Arrow: the spare wheel neatly tucked inside (*J. Brucker, Los Angeles, Ca. Photo: Nicky Wright*)

143

RIGHT: Back view of the 1933
Pierce Silver Arrow (*J.
Brucker, Los Angeles, Ca.
Photo: Nicky Wright*)

Arrow was upholstered in broadcloth, with birdseye maple woodwork; the rear compartment was fitted with a radio and a set of duplicate instruments. The aerodynamic efficiency of its startling coachwork was reflected in a top speed of around 115mph.

There were other 'super-streamlined' cars in the 1930s, like architect Buckminster Fuller's 'geodesic' Dymaxion car, a teardrop-shaped three-wheeler with a rear-mounted Ford V8. Perhaps the most striking of them all was the 'Phantom Corsair' designed by Rust Heinz, son of the canned food king H. J. ('57 Varieties') Heinz, as the prototype for a planned limited production run.

A true 'dream car', the Phantom Corsair was powered by a 4731cc Cord 810 V8 engine driving the front wheels which, like those at the rear, were faired into the bodywork. The futuristic bodywork was built in Pasadena by Bohman and Schwartz and had the lights recessed into the aggressive nose, which had only the smallest possible arrow-shaped cooling louvres disturbing its clean contours. The passenger compartment, soundproofed with cork and rubber, and upholstered in red leather, had a steeply raked two-panel windscreen of exquisite narrowness and seated four abreast (one to the left and two to the right of the driver). The instrument panel contained speedometer, revolution counter, fuel gauge, barometer, compass and battery condition indicator, as well as a radio.

This amazing machine was said to be capable of reaching a top speed of 115mph, and cost $25,000 to construct. Plans for series production of replicas at a price of $12,500 were well in hand when, on 24 July 1939, Rust Heinz was killed in a car accident at the age of twenty-five. But his dream car survives as the centrepiece of a special display of classic cars from Harrah's Auto Museum staged in Dusseldorf, Germany in June 1979 – an exhibition which, by the theatricality of its staging, rivalled the great custom salons of the 1920s. The Phantom Corsair outclassed even the Pierce Silver Arrow, no small feat in such exalted company. It even appeared in the film *The Young in Heart*, proving that, like children and dogs, classic automobiles can always be guaranteed to steal the scene.

BELOW: A 'dream car' of the 1930s, the super-streamlined Phantom Corsair had Cord power and was designed by Rust Heinz (DBW)

8 Sisters

under the Skin

If motoring had an equivalent to the Philosophers' Stone, which legend said could change base metals into gold, it would surely be the astute convertors who took high-performance chassis of humble origins, cloaked them in elegant coachwork that concealed their parentage, and marketed them under new and socially acceptable names. This was an art that dated back to the days of the ubiquitous Model T Ford. Especially in Europe, the racy lines of smart-looking cars like the Goodyear, the TAGA and the DeWandre concealed that, mechanically, they were just the same old Detroit models that millions of less pretentious motorists were driving in its undisguised form – stark, black and spidery.

There were some strange transformations. When Rickenbacker failed in 1927, Jurgen-Skafte Rasmussen, the Danish head of the German DKW concern, bought up much of the production machinery and shipped it to Europe, where he used it to build straight-eight 4872cc Rickenbacker engines for Audi. At the 1929 Paris Salon, it was reported: 'Both the Bollack and the BNC straight-eights are engined by Lycoming. The former is almost entirely built up of American parts, while the latter chassis has independent wheels with pneumatic suspension.' It was added that the radiator design of the Bollack was 'somewhat bizarre . . .'.

The year 1932 really saw the start of a new phase of the transformation game, for in that year two new models emerged from famous mass-production factories with the promise of sports car performance at a family car price. They were the Ford V8 and the Essex Terraplane. Each would be the unwitting progenitor of a classic British marque. Essex had coined the word 'Terraplane' to describe their new six-cylinder range launched in July 1932, with a power unit of 3162cc derived from the larger Pacemaker Six. The idea behind the Terraplane was increased performance through the elimination of surplus weight, 'giving a new freedom, a new comfort and a new safety to high-speed motoring'.

The speed potential of the new model was not lost on the British importing company, a Hudson-Essex subsidiary that assembled the cars in a factory on London's Great West Road. Fired by the parent company's promises that the Terraplane had the best power-to-weight ratio of any car over 12hp built up to that time and would 'wheel and corner like a speed boat, follow its nose round curves with the smooth ease of an aeroplane banking,' they offered as a standard production model two sports derivatives of the Terraplane with special coachwork designed by Windovers. These were a Sports Saloon four-seater, 'built on low sporting lines with adjustable front seats, hand-buffed leather upholstery, sliding roof and roomy luggage compartment' and an Open Sports four-seater, 'extremely smart in design, being modelled along the lines of the racing cars seen at Brooklands, with neatly fitted folded hood, large luggage compartment and upholstery in beautiful hand-buffed leather.' Amazingly, the Windover bodies, embodying the 'craftsmanship that has won Windovers the patronage of those who demand distinctive style and unsurpassed quality of bodywork', cost no more than the mass-produced bodies of the rest of the Terraplane range.

Motor took the Terraplane Sports out on test, noting:

On the road this model is particularly fascinating to handle, for it cruises without fuss and with commendable smoothness at 60mph . . . On Brooklands track, the Essex was remarkably steady, control being effected with only finger-light pressure. There is a complete absence of roll when cornering, and

PAGES 146 AND 147: The 1935 Railton (*Photo: Nicky Wright*)

148

the car is equally stable when it is driven fast against the camber. Steering could not be better or lighter . . .

The Windover Sports did not last long, however, and by the 1933 Olympia Motor Show the firm was back at its normal trade of fitting bespoke bodies to Rolls-Royce and other luxury chassis. In the meantime, the Essex marque had been supplanted by Terraplane and a new straight-eight of 4010cc launched, which gave an 'outstandingly brilliant' performance (and was, apparently, one of the first production cars available with a metallic finish). In Britain, Captain Noel Macklin's Invicta car company was running out of orders due to the Depression, having priced itself out of the market with its high-quality cars which were nevertheless assembled from proprietary components. In fact, the Invicta had quite a bit in common with some of the more exclusive American assembled cars for it had been designed very much as a top-gear machine, intended to have the flexibility of a steam car. It was hardly surprising, therefore, that Captain Macklin looked to an American chassis to save his company and chose the Terraplane Eight, with its 94bhp engine ('Not just a car – a thrilling experience').

BELOW: The mass-produced Essex Terraplane (this 1932 example belonged to Amelia Earhart) was the basis for the British Railton car (DBW)

Others built custom coachwork on the Terraplane chassis – Motor Bodies and Engineering offered a particularly pretty blue-and-aluminium drophead coupé – but Macklin was not just interested in a cosmetic job. Despite the eulogistic road tests, the Terraplane had certain roadholding shortcomings which became all too apparent if it was driven hard. Its soft suspension, suited to American tastes, encouraged the Terraplane to leave the ground when cornered fast, living up to its slogan of 'Land Flying'.

Before production ceased and the marque was acquired by Earl Fitzwilliam, Invicta's last project had been a 5-litre supercharged sports six-cylinder 'to challenge every foreign car in the world'. Macklin wanted the new model to be at least a worthy successor to the Invicta and capable of sustained high speed. He therefore engaged Reid Railton as consulting engineer, who had as much experience of designing high-speed cars as any man in England for he had worked as assistant to Parry Thomas at Leyland in the early 1920s and subsequently became a director of the Brooklands racing engineers, Thomson and Taylor Limited. Railton was best known at that time as the designer of the latest incarnation of Sir Malcolm Campbell's *Blue Bird* land speed record car, and also of John Cobb's big Napier-Railton Brooklands racer with a Napier Lion aeroengine. He was also responsible for the chassis of the ERA racing voiturette.

ABOVE: 1937 Railton with sunroof coachwork (*Photo: Nicky Wright*)

LEFT: A 1937 Railton dashboard panel (*Photo: Nicky Wright*)

ABOVE: 1938 Railton Cobham
Saloon (*National Motor
Museum, Beaulieu*)

Faced with the redesign of the Terraplane, he lowered the centre of
gravity by redesigning the chassis. At the same time, he stiffened up the
suspension, which was fitted with Andre Telecontrol dampers controlled by
the driver, and increased the steering ratio. A handsome radiator shell,
similar to that of the Invicta but vee-fronted, with the rivets down the
bonnet – also a hall-mark of that make – were further distinguishing
touches that set the Railton Terraplane apart from the standard product.
Initially only an open four-seater sports, a coupé and a saloon were offered,
but during 1934 the range of bodies was increased to seven. The 'Terraplane' part of the name was soon dropped, and the car was known simply
as the 'Railton', and advertised as the 'Car Extraordinary', road testers
greeting it with fulsome phrases such as 'the engine even at great road
speeds seems to be idling . . . it will cruise at 75mph without any sensation of
"driving" the car'.

The Terraplane Eight was discontinued in 1934, so the Railton adopted
the similar but slightly larger Hudson Eight (4168cc). The Railton four-
door saloon cost £565 against £385 for the standard Hudson Eight (though
the Hudson Club Saloon, complete with 'generous equipment at six-valve
superhet wireless set', cost £485). The Hudson engine was a somewhat
agricultural unit with splash lubrication, but nevertheless managed to put
out 113bhp at 4000rpm, giving a top speed in the region of 90mph. By
1936 the engine was delivering 124bhp, though the Railton was becoming

ABOVE: 1936 Railton Sports
Tourer by Carbodies
(*National Motor Museum,
Beaulieu*)

more luxurious and therefore needed the extra power to cope with its
increasing weight. By the end of the 1930s, the Railton had become very
much a luxury car, with tourers made only to special order; in 1938 a six-
cylinder variant appeared but found few customers. A total of 1460
Railtons was built, and fourteen were assembled after the war in the
Hudson-Essex factory on the Great West Road using 1939 components.

The Railton was perhaps the most successful of what were unkindly
termed 'Anglo-American Sports Bastards'. There were others, however,
which would outlive Railton and become well-known names in the motor
industry. The Jensen, product of body stylists Richard and Alan Jensen,
grew out of their sports conversion of three 1936 Ford V8-68 chassis (one
of these was shipped to Hollywood, reputedly to the order of Clark Gable
who, though he never owned it, posed for publicity photos beside it). Late
in 1936 Jensens launched a Ford-engined luxury sporting car which
managed fairly successfully to conceal its true parentage. A special, double-
dropped chassis frame brought the car as close to the ground as possible
though it retained Ford's traditional transverse suspension front and rear
('specially laid out,' claimed the Jensens, 'to bring the car low, and to afford
the desirable stability').

The coachwork was particularly special, with a 'decidedly pleasing,
distinctively clean-cut' vee-shaped radiator and sweeping wings. A saloon
and four-seater open tourer were the first models offered, with a coupé

being added in 1937. The stunning looks of the Jensen won many prizes in Concours d'Elegance; but the car could also travel fast and hard. Standard equipment included a Columbia dual-ratio rear axle controlled by a pre-selector switch to the left of the steering column which stepped up the gearing from the normal ratio of 4.1:1 to the very high ratio of 2.9:1 so that, at 60mph in high ratio, the engine was only turning over at 2000rpm. In saloon form, the Jensen could travel at over 80mph, with petrol consumption around 20mpg.

The success of the Jensen formula can be gauged by the impression the car made on *The Autocar*'s road tester:

On a long journey, this proves a remarkably untiring car to handle, which in large measure must be due to the quietness and ease of operation, and also to the ready manner in which the car meets the driver's ideas. In addition, the suspension is extremely comfortable, being practically devoid of any tendency to side roll, and giving exceptional insulation over a bad surface . . . The car can be cornered in the way that is expected of a good quality British car, and also it steers accurately.'

Jensen also offered in 1938 the 22hp Ford V8 engine that had been specifically designed to respond to the European taxes on horsepower; a Nash straight-eight was a subsequent option. But perhaps the most

ABOVE: The elegant good looks of the Ford V8-powered Jensen won many concours awards. This 1938 Tourer had a turbocharger (DBW)

ABOVE RIGHT: Montier of Levallois, Paris, created this straight-eight racer in 1930 using two Model A Ford engines in line (DBW)

BELOW RIGHT: The Batten-Special was an elegant sports car built in Beckenham, Kent, based on the Ford V8 (DBW)

intriguing feature of the 1938 Jensen range was the optional fitment of a turbocharger to the 30hp V8. Running at seven times crankshaft speed, the turbocharger operated 'practically without noise', yet gave the car similar acceleration in overdrive top as it had unblown in the 'normal' ratio. 'Quiet and smooth and generally handling like a thoroughbred', the Jensen was perhaps Britain's closest approach to the American concept of a classic car, especially when it was fitted with 'dual-cowl' tourer bodywork.

have already pointed out, after Novem- there will be no speed limit for the motorist. Whilst this means that an restriction is removed, *it does not a motorist as fast as without the conse- The old ons*

been in- There can

certificate of insurance. This certificate (which

Contd. Page 786.

IN THE GRAND PRIX D' EUROPE.
One of two Ford cars that challenged well-known racing cars in the famous European race. This car completed the course of 370 miles at an average speed of over 65 m.p.h. with a petrol consumption of 22 miles per gallon.

783

155

After the war, Jensen switched its allegiance to British power units but one constructor who remained faithful to the big V8s was Sydney Allard, who built his first Allard Special in 1936. He built a few elegant sports cars with Ford V8 engines before the war, though the heyday of the stark and sporty Allard was to be in the late 1940s and early 1950s.

The Batten-Special, originating from a V8 specially built for competition work, was a handsome car from Kent available either as an open tourer or as a coupé. But it did not have the panache of the Allard and consequently was in production only from 1935 to 1938. Other British marques of the 1930s used the Ford V8 engine, among them such obscurities as the Leidart, the Nunn (a sporting saloon built by a Ford dealership) and the superlatively hideous Fitzmaurice Special, a bulbous streamlined model with horizontal louvres all round its bonnet, *à la* Cord.

On the other hand, when George Brough, maker of one of Britain's best-loved big-twin sporting motorcycles, decided to branch out into car production, he went for straight-six and -eight power units (also used in several Allards and possibly one or two Jensens). His Brough-Superior cars all used Hudson engines except for the very last one, which had a Lincoln-Zephyr V12. The latter unit also found its way into some of the all-

BELOW: 1935 Brough Superior (*National Motor Museum, Beaulieu*)

independently suspended Atalanta sports cars built between 1937 and 1939 as an alternative to the troublesome Gough 1½- and 2-litre engines. The 4.3 litre Lincoln-Zephyr unit at least gave this intriguing sports car (in which A. C. Bertelli, late of Aston Martin, was involved) more exciting performance, even if it didn't do a lot for reliability.

The Lammas-Graham was just as ill-starred. It used the supercharged Graham 3.7 litre six which was built in chassis form at Sunbury-on-Thames, Middlesex, ready for bodywork by Abbott, Bertelli or Carlton. Despite its rapid 128bhp engine, the Lammas-Graham looked so staid – rather like an Armstrong-Siddeley, in fact – that it appealed neither to sportsman nor socialite.

ABOVE: A 1952 Allard P1 Saloon beside Buttermere (*National Motor Museum, Beaulieu*)

9 The Tin-Tops

take over

In the 1920s and early 1930s the limited production luxury cars tended to set the pace for the American industry, because it was generally the wealthy who could afford to pay the price of new technology. Take, for instance, the case of synchromesh, which was invented and patented by Earl A. Thompson in 1926. He devised a system in which friction cones synchronized the speeds of the revolving gear wheels and remained in action for a time controlled by 'an ingenious hydraulic dashpot device', after which a dog clutch engaged the gears. He took his invention to General Motors who, although interested, could find no way of producing the new gearbox cheaply. So they made Thompson assistant chief engineer of Cadillac and in 1929 the Thompson Syncro-Mesh gearbox appeared on Cadillacs, the only models in the GM range which could stand the extra cost. Having secured the kudos of being first in the field, GM then set its engineering staffs to developing a cheaper form of syncromesh, which duly appeared on Buick cars in 1931.

As the 1930s progressed and America began to climb out of recession, it became obvious that the advanced ideas were now coming largely from the mass producers in their ever fiercer battle to capture the customers. In 1933 Reo was the first manufacturer to offer an automatic transmission, a two-speed epicyclic unit controlled by a centrifugal clutch which auto-

PAGES 158 AND 159: This is the 1940 version of the Lincoln Zephyr V12 sedan, designed by E. T. Gregorie (*R. Schirmer, Auburn-Cord-Duesenberg Museum. Photo: Nicky Wright*)

BELOW: 1936 Ford Station Wagon (*Val Danneskold, Cal. Photo: Nicky Wright*)

matically shifted from low to high ratio at about 12mph: 'The gearing is so quiet and the transition so gentle that the change of speed ratio occurs almost without the driver being aware of the fact,' wrote an entranced journalist. Reo's transmission was really a 2 × 2-speed with two gears in high and low ranges. The normal shift from 'hi' to 'lo' and *vice versa* was fully automatic, but to get from high to low range or low to high, you not only had to de-clutch, but double de-clutch as there was no synchromesh.

Chrysler, always the most 'engineering-minded' of the mass producers, offered on its late 1932 models 'Floating Power' flexible engine suspension, an automatic clutch operated by engine suction, a free-wheel unit and all-steel bodywork welded to form a unit with the chassis. General Motors was particularly fortunate in having a range of products which went right across the market, from Chevrolet at the lower end to Cadillac in the highest price range. This meant that it could carry out a continuous research programme with the cost spread across the various GM lines, and that the result of that research could be introduced into production on a model at the appropriate price level.

As far back as 1920, the General Motors Research Corporation was investigating new forms of transmission, initially concentrating on electric transmissions then, from about 1923, investigating infinitely variable automatic transmissions. Eventually a steel-on-steel friction drive was devised and handed over to Buick to evaluate in 1928 with a view to putting it into production four years later. But there proved to be too many built-in problems, and the search for an automatic transmission was turned over to Cadillac who, by 1934, were on the path that would lead to the Hydra-Matic, the first successful mass-production automatic transmission.

Cadillac were also continuing their investigation of suspension characteristics and early in 1932 decided that the time was ripe to begin work on independent front suspension systems, as there was a limit to the softness of ride that could be obtained with a conventional beam axle above which handling was greatly impaired. Ernest Seaholm and Maurice Olley built two experimental Cadillacs, one with Dubonnet-type independent front suspension, the other using a 'wishbone' suspension developed by the GM engineers. Independent rear suspension was also fitted on these two mobile test rigs.

In March 1933, the engineers were ready to show their new developments to the top management. GM's general technical committee assembled at the Cadillac engineering building for a test run in the two Cadillacs, and a Buick with infinitely variable automatic transmission. GM head Alfred P. Sloan and sales vice-president Dick Grant climbed into the 'wishbone' car and set off into the Detroit traffic. Two miles out, Seaholm and Olley, in a support car, pulled up alongside the Cadillac at a traffic light. Sloan and Grant were smiling broadly at one another, and Sloan was moving the flat of his hand up and down and horizontally to demonstrate the effectiveness of the new suspension system.

After the demonstration runs, Grant's reaction was immediate: 'A hundred dollars for an automatic transmission is something a Buick buyer can well do without, but if I could have a ride like you've shown us for a matter of fifteen bucks, I'd find the money somehow!' So at the 1934 Motor Show, Cadillac, Oldsmobile and Buick had the wishbone front suspension and Chevrolet and Pontiac had a Dubonnet-type ifs system, though this was eventually dropped in favour of wishbones. 'It seems to me we can't afford *not* to do it!' had been GM's engineering genius 'Boss'

The 1939 Graham Sharknose
(*Cliff Shepler, Ca. Photo:
Nicky Wright*)

Kettering's reaction to independent front suspension. But the secret of GM's success was that they *could* afford to take radical steps of this kind.

They could also afford to offer prestigious loss-leaders like the V12 and V16 Cadillacs, which were produced up to 1937, when they were dropped in favour of a new V16, again the work of Ernest Seaholm. This had only half the number of moving parts as its predecessor, largely because it had a sidevalve layout against the ohv of the original V16; the cylinder blocks were set at the unusually wide angle of 135 degrees. Just 511 of this new V16 were built between 1938 and 1940, against 3863 of the original model.

Meanwhile Cadillac had been carrying out a steady programme of model development under the guidance of German-born Nicholas Dreystadt, who took over as general manager in 1934. In 1935 a new V8 engine of 5676cc was introduced alongside the old 5275cc unit; being made largely of cast iron, it was cheaper to produce. Even so, *The Autocar* remarked: 'The make is specially notable for the high external finish given to the engine, so that when the bonnet is opened the effect produced is comparable with that applying to a high-grade European car'. This larger engine was common to all 1937 eight-cylinder cars and standardized on all Cadillacs by 1941, in which year the Hydra-Matic automatic transmission was available as an option. This was the first time a luxury car had been equipped with an automatic gearbox, though a semi-automatic had made its debut on the 1938 model Buick and Oldsmobile, the latter marque being chosen in October 1939 for the first fully automatic Hydra-Matic.

By that time, it had become apparent that LaSalle had come to the end of its road. It was offered with a straight-eight engine from 1934 to 1937, but in the latter year the LaSalle had reverted to a V8, though it now shared a common bodyshell with Buick and Oldsmobile. Sales figures proved that in this case three models sharing one body was too much, and in 1940 the LaSalle was dropped. (In 1929–30, GM had attempted to market a lower-priced V8, the Olds-built Viking, which had quickly been consigned to Valhalla when it failed to sell.)

Cadillac, however, went from strength to strength, mainly due to the talents of Harley Earl, who had been appointed head of the new 'Art and Colour Section' in 1927, which was the nucleus of the GM Styling Division. By the 1930s he was heading a staff of 450, advising all the GM divisions on the appearance of their products.

Earl's philosophy was simple: 'My primary purpose . . . was to lengthen and lower the American automobile, at times in reality and always in appearance. Why? Because my sense of proportion tells me that oblongs are more attractive than squares . . .' He was also concerned with integrating the excrescences on the average GM car, hiding petrol tanks under a 'beaver tail' skirting and, on the 1932 Cadillacs, providing a built-in luggage boot. Earl made use of advancing technology in the production of sheet steel (which became available for the first time in strips as wide as 80in) to change from composite roofs with a rubberized fabric centre section to all-steel 'turret tops' on GM's 1935 models. For the first time, a roof panel could be stamped from a single piece of steel.

In 1938 the Cadillac 60-Special appeared, a de luxe version of the normal product which carried a price premium, for GM claimed that this was 'the first modern mass-production car to eliminate the running board,' so that a full-width six-seater body could be used. It was also the first car with 'hard-top' styling. Harley Earl was appointed a vice-president of General Motors in 1940, the first stylist ever to hold such a major position, emphasizing the importance that styling had assumed in corporate thinking. It was also at this period that the first 'dream car' was created by the GM styling staff. The purpose of this 1937 'Y-Job', which was built by Buick, was to act as a testbed for new styling and engineering concepts which might find their way on to future production models. The 'Y-Job' incorporated such radical ideas as a full-width grille, retractable headlamps and an electrically-operated hood.

The value of Harley Earl's styling skills to GM was amply proven when, in conjunction with the talented young head of the Cadillac studio, William Mitchell, he created a new look for Cadillac with an 'egg-crate' grille design which was to be a continuing feature of the marque. Sales responded by rising to an all-time high of 66,130.

Chrysler responded to the dream-car concept by commissioning two special limited-production models from LeBaron, which created a great stir in 1941 and have since come to be regarded as classics, though neither had much influence on the shape of Chryslers to come. One of these 1941 LeBarons, the Newport, was an intriguing blend of ancient and modern, a dual-cowl phaeton with full-width styling and concealed rear wings. Only five were built; from the front they looked rather like a sleeping doll, with a narrow 'nose' grille and wide 'mouth' grille and pop-up headlamps in either wing.

The other of these limited-run Chryslers was the Thunderbolt, a bulbous device with all four wheels concealed inside the full-width wings and a steel hardtop over the driving compartment which flipped back into the boot, completely hidden from sight, when the car was converted into an open two-seater. Just six Thunderbolts were built. They were only marginally less ugly than the controversial Chrysler Airflow range of 1934–37.

The mass-producers did not have it all their own way when it came to pioneering radical styling for in 1933 Gordon Miller Buehrig, chief body designer of Duesenberg, was charged with the creation of a new lower-priced 'Baby Duesenberg' that would be a possible successor to the J and

SJ, whose sales were beginning to tail off. Buehrig had a pet project in mind – a radically different concept of automobile styling that he had entered in a design contest organized by Harley Earl. This had no conventional radiator grille, but a 'coffin nose' with all-round horizontal louvres and twin radiators mounted in the airstream between the bonnet and the pontoon wings, which incorporated retractable headlights. A mock-up body was mounted on an Auburn chassis, and Buehrig patented this 'new, original and ornamental design for an automobile' shortly before he was transferred to Auburn for some emergency restyling of the range to stimulate sales. Here he created the dashingly vulgar Auburn 851 Speedster, available with a supercharger installation designed by Augie-Duesenberg. It came with four gargantuan flexible exhaust pipes emerging from the bonnet side and developed some 150bhp against the 115bhp of the unblown model. Every 851 Speedster and its 1936 successor, the 852, carried a dashboard plaque stating that it had been tested at over 100mph. But these eye-catching cars failed to save Auburn from closure in 1936.

On his return to the Baby Duesenberg project, Buehrig learned that it was now to be built as a Cord, with front-wheel drive, though Erret Lobban Cord's vacillating enthusiasm for the project meant that a definite decision to proceed with the new Cord came only four months before the New York Motor Show, where it was intended to launch the car. To qualify for exhibition, a hundred examples of a new car had to have been built, and it was only by a concerted effort that the Cord staff managed to turn out a hundred hand-built cars in time.

Adding to their problems was the fact that the Auburn-Cord-Duesenberg group was desperately short of funds, so every possible saving had to be made in designing the new model for production. Only two door dies were used on four-door models (right front and left rear) and an extra cutter die used to stamp out the cutouts for the rear wheels; the roof on closed models had to be welded up from separate panels because Auburn-Cord-Duesenberg did not possess a large enough press. Interior door handles were bought cheaply at a bankruptcy sale and fitted with showy plastic knobs and the instruments were also acquired cheaply though Buehrig's aircraft-style dashboard made them look very expensive.

Other features of the Cord included the retractable headlamps, which were actually landing lights from Stinson aircraft, built by another of Cord's companies, which had to be cranked up and down manually, and a 4730cc Lycoming V8. The hundred cars were built in time for the New York Show, but lacked the front-wheel drive transmission, which was still undergoing development. This seemed needlessly complex considering the short development timescale and the company's financial weakness, for it featured electro-pneumatic selection of the gears controlled by a miniature lever moving in a gate on the steering column.

Unfortunately for Cord, the car proved an immediate success, and many orders were taken at the Show with delivery promised for Christmas. But those hopeful customers only received a tiny scale model of the Cord mounted on a block of marble. Unlike the Chrysler Airflow, the unorthodox styling of the Cord did not frighten the customers away but positively encouraged them. Even *The Autocar*'s 'hard-boiled critics', the writer Montague Tombs and the artist F. Gordon Crosby:

instantly met the Cord, not with contumely, but with a real appreciation of a fine piece of bold and original designing work . . . falling to unalloyed apprecia-

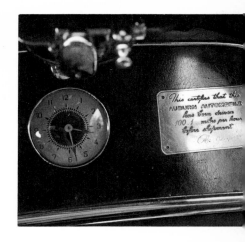

ABOVE: Every supercharged Auburn Speedster carried a dashboard plaque attesting that Ab Jenkins had driven it over 100mph (*Auburn-Cord-Duesenberg Museum. Photo: Nicky Wright*)

OPPOSITE ABOVE: David Abbot ('Ab') Jenkins, the famous Mormon racing driver, (left) in front of the A-C-D building with a 1935 Auburn Cabriolet (*Auburn-Cord-Duesenberg Museum*)

OPPOSITE BELOW: An early example of the 1935 Auburn 851 four-door phaeton, a sporting machine with a 115bhp power unit (*Auburn-Cord-Duesenberg Museum*)

ABOVE: The Chrysler De Soto Airflow range of 1934–37 was aerodynamically efficient but aesthetically awful . . . (*Photo : Nicky Wright*)

OPPOSITE ABOVE: Supercharged Auburn Speedster (*Auburn-Cord-Duesenberg Museum. Photo : Nicky Wright*)

OPPOSITE BELOW: 1935 Auburn Model 851 Phaeton Sedan, bodied by Central. (*Don Allison, Auburn-Cord-Duesenberg Museum. Photo : Nicky Wright*)

tion of original work, not forgetting the clever details of the trap-doors for lamps in the streamline wings, and the manner in which the bottom edges of the wings are not left straight down, but are neatly turned inwards. It was agreed that this treatment of wings . . . is one of the best improvements in artistic detail of the year.

If the Cord had been produced with a conventional transmission, it might have stood some chance of success but the development problems slowed production to about a twelfth of the planned target. Only 1174 were registered on the home market and early examples of the 4730cc Lycoming V8 suffered from overheating and cracked cylinder-heads. Moreover, even when the unorthodox transmission was sorted out, it was found that it took the edge off the Cord's performance for there was a definite delay between

ABOVE: Three detail views of the 1937 Cord Sportsman (*Auburn-Cord-Duesenberg Museum. Photo : Nicky Wright*)

the selection of the gear and its engagement. By this time, Erret Lobban Cord was disenchanted with the auto industry. In 1936 he sold his major holdings in the Auburn-Cord-Duesenberg group for $4 million and went off to Nevada the following year to pursue a new-found interest in radio and television.

Faced with financial disaster in 1937, the Auburn-Cord-Duesenberg management applied their classic formula in times of trouble: supercharge it and fit outside exhaust pipes. The new Model 812 was therefore optionally equipped with a Schwitzer-Cummins turbocharger running at six times crankshaft speed, and positively driven by gearing from the crankshaft (though a slipper mechanism was incorporated in the blower drive to prevent the gear teeth from stripping at full load). As introduced, the supercharged Cord engine developed 170bhp; later blown Cord power units ran up to 195bhp, and 200bhp-plus was possible on a well-tuned example. Ab Jenkins calculated that the maximum power unit was 225bhp, and claimed to have reached 121mph with a blown Cord, which he said would have averaged 120mph on the salt if he had been allowed to fit racing tyres for record attempts instead of the standard units which threw treads at speed.

The Cord's market was necessarily limited; it cost twice as much as a Cadillac and about five times as much as a Ford. As a sop to the luxury market, a long wheelbase 'Custom' model was launched in 1937. Longer and higher than the normal models, the Custom Cords offered more interior room, while the Custom Berline had a wind-up glass division behind the front seat, radio loudspeakers in the rear compartment and an electric telephone for communicating with the chauffeur.

Some 1937 Cords were, as an experiment, bodied by LeBaron with 'conventional' radiator grilles, bonnets and running boards. Fortunately for the Cord's image these lumpish devices did not pass the pilot build stage, though at least one survives today. They were tangible evidence that the Auburn-Cord-Duesenberg empire had lost its way; bereft of Erret Cord's leadership, it was slowly failing. Duesenberg's end had been signalled in 1935, when Lycoming had built the final twenty-five Model J engines and then stopped any further production of this unit as the company had no future sales programme. The last appearance of a Duesenberg at a motor show was in November 1936 at the New York Show; it was not long after that Duesenberg production was officially curtailed and the plant sold to Marmon-Herrington. The last Duesenberg, with a special radiator cowling and Rollston cabriolet body, was assembled in Chicago by August Duesenberg after the plant had closed down and was sold to a wealthy German customer.

Only Cord was now left and, ironically, 1937 was not too bad a year with enough Cords being sold to bring total production to 2320 in just under two years. Then production ended. In 1938, the tattered remains of Auburn-Cord-Duesenberg were sold for what they would fetch to Dallas E. Winslow of Detroit and a spares and service operation for the three marques was set up in Auburn, Indiana.

But the story was not quite over. Hupmobile (whose straight-eights — recalled one 1930s owner — gave smoothness and reliability equal to the family's Rolls-Royce 20/25) was at its last gasp and for its 1939 range bought the body dies for the Cord 810/812 and adapted the design for rear-wheel drive. To enable Hupmobile to recoup some cash by letting off large areas of their large factory, Graham built Hupmobile's Cord-bodied Skylarks, fitted with engine, brakes and, possibly, transmissions made in the part of the Hupmobile factory that the company had retained. In return for this, Graham had the right to use the Hupmobile chassis body with their own engine and sell it as the Graham Hollywood. Production of both types ceased about Summer 1940. Hupmobile gave up car manufacture in 1940, moving into car spares, kitchen equipment and electronics.

Only a few months after the Auburn-Cord-Duesenberg group had received its final quietus another of the great marques, Pierce-Arrow, had staggered to a halt. In 1935 Pierce-Arrow had sold only 1000 cars, yet at the end of the year introduced three outstanding new models, billed as 'the safest cars in the world'. There were two twelve-cylinder models, Models 1602 and 1603, plus an eight (Model 1601). Prices started at $3195, yet these cars offered such features as powerful vacuum-servo brakes, anti-roll bar on the rear suspension, massive X-braced chassis, quadruple head-lamps, twin rear lamps, reversing lights, tinted safety glass, crankcase emission control and overdrive. To bolster themselves against financial loss, Pierce-Arrow began to build trailer caravans; but in 1938 an insistent creditor demanded that the company be liquidated to pay off the $200,000 he was owed. Put up to auction, the company's assets, valued at $1 million fetched . . . $40,000. The engine-making machinery was sold to the Seagrave Fire Apparatus Company, so Pierce-Arrow engines continued to give sterling service in Seagrave fire engines for many more years. Pierce-Arrow designer Karl Wise had the last car the company built; one more was to be built from spare parts in 1941, and averaged out as '1934' for registration purposes by its constructors.

The year 1938 also saw the end of two of the great names in coachbuilding, Rollston and Willoughby. There was to be no reprieve for Willoughby, which had relied on Lincoln after all its other clients had failed, only to fade away when orders for coachbuilt Lincolns also dried up. But for Rollston, which declared bankruptcy in April 1938, there was to be an afterlife. Of the 654 custom bodies built by Rollston during its life, 512 were built before the end of 1931, and only 142 in the remaining seven years. But the management thought there was still some hope for the future, and formed a new company, Rollson, Inc. Up to December 1941, they built fifty custom bodies, forty-eight of them on Packard chassis. After the war, nobody wanted custom coachwork, so Rollson diverged into the manufacture of kitchen equipment.

The late 1930s, however, were not entirely gloomy for the makers of prestige automobiles. Packard had come through the Depression remarkably well, and as early as 1933 had made the decision to move down into a lower price bracket without sullying the Packard name. The lessons of the unfortunate Light Eight had been well learnt, and production expert George Christopher was wooed away from GM's Buick and Pontiac Divisions to head the project, which was housed in a separate factory across the way from Packard's main plant. More experts skilled in building 'down to a price' were hired, and in 1934 the first news of the forthcoming medium-priced Packard began to be released to the public, who were so enthusiastic about the whole project that by January 1935, Packard had taken $10 million in cash orders for a car the public had not even seen.

On 6 January 1935, listeners to Lawrence Tibbett's popular radio show heard the first broadcast on the new Packard 120 (the figure was derived from its wheel-base). Later the same week, the 35th Automobile National Show opened in New York under the auspices of the Automobile Merchants Association of New York, the manufacturers' association having decided to wait until the following November for their next show in response to a general feeling that this would help to reduce unemployment in the motor industry during the winter. Packard noted with satisfaction that 10,000 orders had been received for the new 120 range. whose price range started at $980 for the Business Coupé and rose to $1095 for the Touring Sedan. By the end of September, 24,995 examples of the 120 had been sold, putting Packard back into the black. Sales of the costlier Packards held up remarkably well, the 120 poaching few customers from the rest of the firm's line-up. The Twelfth Series Eight, current from

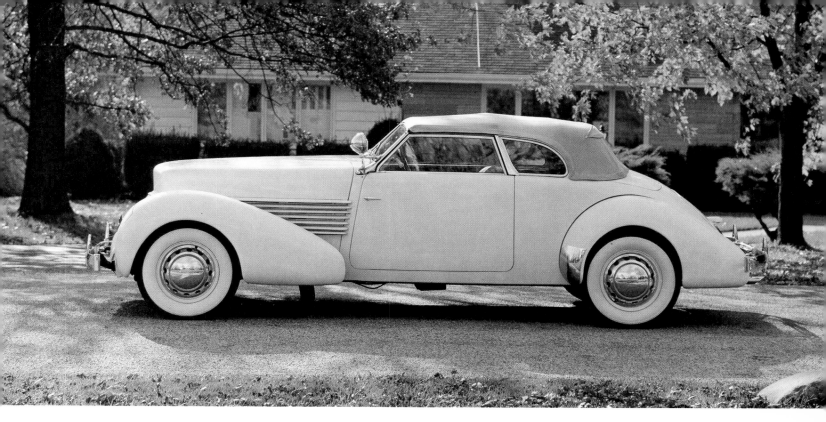

August 1934 to August 1935, sold 4781 examples against 5120 for the
Eleventh Series built over the previous twelve months; for the Super
Eight, the figures were 1392 against 1920, and for the Twelve, 720 Twelfth
Series were built against 960 Eleventh.

The 120 was the first Packard with independent front suspension; the
more expensive models retained beam axles, though they did benefit from
some engine redesign work which boosted power output, the Twelve now
developing around 200bhp. The Twelve also had an ingenious self-cleaning
oil filter which anticipated the Second World War's aircraft practice.
Though the Twelfth Series Eight, Super Eight and Twelve featured new,
more streamlined styling, there were now no true semi-custom bodies on
offer; the so-called 'LeBaron' and 'Dietrich' bodies were actually stock
Briggs and Murray bodies with better trim and a fancy body plate. Full
custom bodies were still available from Rollston, Derham or Brunn, though

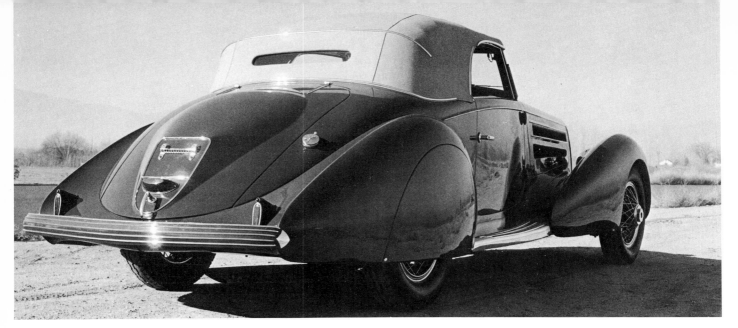

ABOVE: Model J Duesenberg
with body by Graber of
Switzerland (*Harrah's, Reno,
Nevada. Photo : Nicky
Wright*)

RIGHT: Dashboard of the
Graber-bodied Model J
Duesenberg (*Harrah's, Reno,
Nevada. Photo : Nicky Wright*)

the changing financial climate meant that few such orders were placed.

Packard, flushed with success over the 120, decided to bring out a further low-priced model, this time to fall within the $750 price limit, which at that time accounted for 95 per cent of sales. The result was the 110, the first six-cylinder Packard since 1928. At the time of its introduction in September 1936, Packard had 5100 employees, of whom 2500 built 5985 Senior Packards in the old factory that year, and 2600 were in the new factory and built 55,042 of the 120 model, some indication of the relative values attached to the two product lines.

The 110 was a tremendous success and 65,400 were sold during the 1937 season, along with 50,100 of the sister 120 eight, putting Packard in fifth place in overall sales that year. The 1937 Senior Packards had a new look, too. The old Eight and Super Eight had been discontinued, as had Bijur centralized chassis lubrication, beam front axle, optional wire or wood wheels, ride control and vibration-damping bumpers. Now there was just a new, but less powerful, Super Eight using Twelve body components on a new, lighter chassis. The Twelve also had a new chassis with independent front suspension, and was to enjoy its best year ever for sales (as did the entire Packard range) with 1300 cars produced in the season. In all, 122,593 Packards were sold during the 1937 model year.

The following season saw a change of emphasis, with the 110 and 120 redesigned and upgraded in price, and renamed Packard Six and Packard Eight; they were promoted as 'the Six and Eight for Thirty-Eight'. Market research had prompted this regrading, but the economy was on the slide again, losing some two-thirds of the ground it had regained during the five years of Roosevelt's 'New Deal' in nine months; the automobile industry lost 40 per cent in total output that year compared with 1937. For Packard, the recession meant a loss of 62,826 sales compared with the year before. Sales of Super Eight and Twelve were more than halved, to 2478 against 5793 and 566 against 1300 respectively.

In fact, if Packard had not brought out the 110 and 120 when it did, it could well have followed Auburn-Cord-Duesenberg and Pierce-Arrow into extinction at that time. That it did not is due to the good taste and sound business sense of Alvan Macaulay, who was to remain President of Packard until 1942, when he became Chairman, retiring in 1948. He was also President of the Automobile Manufacturers' Association for seventeen years, and President of the Automotive Council for War Production during the Second World War. Chameleon-like, Packard was changing its image to suit the economic climate. Its 1937–38 Sixteenth Series marked a watershed, for it saw the last of the true Super Eights and the last of the superlative semi-custom bodies, Brunn's Cabriolet Touring and Cabriolet All-Weather. These were the most expensive semi-custom Packards of all time, catalogued at $8510, and only thirty-five were built in the 1937–38 period.

The 1938–39 Seventeenth Series Packard range saw the revival of the 120, as the Super Eight was now just the last season's Eight with the old Super Eight engine, and $336 cheaper in its most expensive form than the lowest-priced Sixteenth Series Super Eight. Sales of 3962 against the old model's 2478 the previous year proved the wisdom of the new policy, for this was the only model line of the Seventeenth Series to show a sales increase over its predecessor; sales of the Six were down to 24,350, and the 120 sold 17,647 against the Sixteenth Series Eight's 22,624. The Twelve continued virtually unchanged from the previous series, and, still available with the Brunn Cabriolet bodies, was in its final season, during which only 446 were sold. Packard had successfully established itself as a leading maker of medium-priced cars. The last Packards that were considered as classics were the 180 models of 1940–42; this was an upmarket version of the new 160 eight-cylinder, with which it had engine and body in common. It was on this model that 'Dutch' Darrin, who had forsaken Paris for Hollywood in 1937, created some handsome semi-customs, his Convertible Sedan body having more than a hint of Cord 810 styling about it. But in 1939 the semi-custom business was dying, and Darrin closed down his Hollywood operation, and moved to Detroit as a Packard special body designer for semi-custom bodies built in the Packard works.

Semi-custom bodies were offered on the 180 until America went to war in 1942: but a sign of the future was given in 1941 when stylist Edward Macauley (Alvan Macauley's son) designed an experimental car known as the Packard Phantom, which would become the basis for the postwar Packards. It had a bulbous, full-width body, 'mouth-organ' grille across the full front of the bonnet and wings, quad headlamps and a generally over-blown appearance. It was certainly forward-looking; it was equally certainly the ugliest car Packard had yet built. Worse was to come.

A strategic but stylish retreat downmarket was also the salvation of

ABOVE: 'Rolls-Royce smooth'
– the 1932 Hupmobile 8-22
straight-eight sedan (*Paul
Lavergne, Fort Wayne, Ind.
Photo: Nicky Wright*)

Lincoln. If that company hadn't been backed by Ford in general and Edsel Ford in particular, it would have been closed down in 1931–32. Indeed, Henry Ford's lieutenant, 'Cast Iron' Charlie Sorensen, was all ready to give Lincoln the *coup de grâce*, for sales were virtually static.

Then Briggs, who were regarded by Sorensen as not paying enough attention to their Ford business (he felt they gave too much time to Chrysler) brought in a young Dutch-born designer called John Tjaarda, who had entered an intriguing design for Harley Earl's design contest that had also sired the Cord, the Pierce Silver Arrow and the V16 Cadillac shown at the Chicago Century of Progress exhibition. Tjaarda's concept

ABOVE: A 1941 Graham Hollywood, built using the body dies of the Cord 810, with a 3569cc six (*W. Graham, Auburn-Cord-Duesenberg Museum. Photo: Nicky Wright*)

was a unit-construction streamlined car, and Briggs began developing this concept as a possible lower-priced replacement for the KB Lincoln. A rear-engined mock-up was built, and shown at 'clinics' (some of the first of their kind) round the country to gauge customer reaction. They did not care too much for the rear engine, so two front-engined prototypes were built, using a modified Ford V8 engine.

The Ford management approved this concept, but insisted on some retrograde mechanical features, like live axles and mechanical brakes; Edsel Ford called in Bob Gregorie to tighten up the front-end styling, though Tjaarda's sloping rear deck lines remained similar to those of the proto-

types. Edsel ordered Lincoln's chief engineer to design a more powerful engine for this new model, the result being a V12 of 4387cc with a stunning performance but an unhappy tendency to lubrication problems if it was not scrupulously cared for.

Launched in November 1935 as the Lincoln Zephyr, the new car was an instant success. Of a total of 18,994 Lincolns sold in 1936, no less than 17,715 were Lincoln Zephyrs. 'From all points of view a remarkable car has been produced,' eulogized *The Autocar*. Next year, the Lincoln-Zephyr excelled itself with sales of 25,186. Compare that with the patrician Model K, which sold just 120 in its last two seasons, 1939–40, despite patronage from FDR himself.

The arrival of the Lincoln Zephyr enabled Bob Gregorie to fulfil a personal ambition: to put into production a limited edition car in the idiom of the European-type sporting cars he had created for Edsel Ford's personal use since 1932. Taking a Lincoln Zephyr Convertible Coupé, Gregorie gave it a long, low look by the simple expedient of cutting a four-inch strip out of doors and body side panels. The prototype 'Continental' was ready in 1939, and shipped to Edsel's Florida holiday home for his approval. The lithe grey car created such a sensation wherever it was seen that Edsel decided that it should certainly go into production that October. Using production parts, but virtually hand-built, the Lincoln Continental, distinguished by its vertically-mounted spare tyre at the rear of the body, was described by architect Frank Lloyd Wright as 'the most beautiful car ever built'.

'No other car so satisfied my soul,' author John Steinbeck said of the Continental, and it was to be chosen by the New York Metropolitan Museum of Art in 1951 as one of eight cars which 'excelled as works of art'.

More prosaically, *Time* magazine, in a 1959 listing, ranked the original Lincoln Continental sixth among 'the hundred best-designed commercial products of recent times'.

The original Lincoln Continental design straddled the war years: a total of 5322 was produced in 1940–42 and 1946–48. Of these, 2277 were cabriolets and 3045 coupés. The Lincoln Continental outlasted both its progenitors. Production of the true Lincoln Zephyr ended in 1942, and though the postwar Lincoln used the Zephyr bodyshell, the front-end styling had become heavy and vulgar, with an ugly grille.

That was probably inevitable for, in 1943, Edsel Ford had died, aged only forty-nine. No single man, perhaps, had done more to create the classic American automobile. Ray Dietrich described Edsel as 'a gentleman . . . with cultured taste and good judgment.' His passing left a void that could not be filled and, in Dietrich's opinion, 'a heritage no-one could touch'.

10 Aftermath

The shape of the postwar American car was decided one day during the war when an Air Force friend of Harley Earl's was rash enough to show the GM designer a top secret fighter aircraft, the Lockheed P-38 Lightning. This was a flying gun platform with twin Allison engines mounted on twin tail booms, each ending in a rounded fin.

Earl thought it was one of the most exciting things he had seen and sought security clearance for his design staff so that they could view those tail fins too. They were, reportedly, as interested by the Lightning as Earl, and their design sketches dutifully began to feature cars with tail fins within months. (This was nothing new; after the Great War, the Dutch Spyker company had built 'aerocoque' sports cars with aircraft type empennage to the design of aeronautical engineer Fritz Koolhoven.)

The first postwar Cadillacs were merely a continuation of the rounded contours of the 1942 line. In 1948 the first Cadillacs with tail fins appeared amid a storn of controversy. They seemed to be part of a campaign of deliberate 'uglification' which was to make the 'Caddys' of the 1950s, with their Flash Gordon spaceship fins and heavy jowls, some of the most hideous vehicles spawned in an era of poor taste, an era in which tailfins sprouted on most popular models.

Nearly all the cars of that time seemed to have been created in the jelly-mould of fashion. Few of the immediately postwar cars were truly attractive though some, like Chrysler's Town and Country series (launched in 1941 as a station wagon) with its external wood framing and appliqué woodgrain side panelling, had a certain curiousity value.

There were, admittedly, a few notable custom vehicles. In 1948 Louis Fageol of the Twin Coach company built a streamlined car called 'Supersonic', powered by an all-alloy 275bhp engine with an overhead camshaft, fuelled by liquid petroleum gas. With faired-in front wheels, the Supersonic was said to be capable of 150mph, and was regularly used on long trips from Fageol's base in Kent, Ohio, to both New York and California. There was also designer Alex Tremulis's Torpedo Grand Sport, a modern dual cowl phaeton designed for steel magnate Henry J. Kaiser's Kaiser marque, launched after the war in a brave attempt to match the Big Three. Kaiser did market several hundred examples of a glass fibre bodied sportster designed by Dutch Darrin, and generally known as the 'Kaiser-Darrin'.

For Packard, which had survived the vicissitudes of the 1930s and made a major contribution to America's war effort, peace had brought only problems. As a gesture towards Soviet-American friendship while the two great powers were allies during the war, President Roosevelt had requested Packard to sell the body dies of the 160/180 range to the Russians at a nominal price. The Russians produced the Packard model after the war as the ZIS (Zavod Imieni Stalina). All Packard had for immediate postwar production was the medium-priced Clipper eight. There was no luxury model to compete with Lincoln and Cadillac for that section of the car-hungry postwar market that wanted a high-priced vehicle and there was not enough steel allocated to Packard for it to meet demand for Clippers, now renamed Twenty-first Series and available in Six, Super Eight and Custom Super models (only Eights were built in 1945, just 2722 of them, but the full range was offered in 1946–47).

So Packard, which had planned to build 100,000 cars in its first full year of postwar production, was unable to build more than 42,102 in 1946 and 55,477 in 1947. Production of the first true postwar model, the Twenty-Second Series, started in August 1947. This model was based on Ed

Macauley's prewar 'dream car' and its bloated styling earned it such nicknames as the 'Pregnant Elephant' and the 'Inverted Bathtub'. It must be recorded, however, that the Twenty-Second Series, which had cost Packard some $15 million in development costs, sold very well. Packard was back on target in 1948, with almost 99,000 cars sold while 1949 was the company's second-best year for sales with 104,593 Packards registered, and a Packard-developed automatic transmission introduced.

In March 1951 Packard brought out the unfortunate Twenty-Fourth Series whose 'contour styling' and gaping grille gave it the appearance of something trawled up from the ocean floor. Sales began to slip and in

TOP: This is the 1948 Lincoln Continental Convertible owned by Hollywood star Clark Gable (DBW)

BELOW: The 1948 Lincoln V12 Continental (*Auburn-Cord-Duesenberg Museum. Photo: Nicky Wright*)

ABOVE: 1953 Buick Skylark.
50th anniversary model
(*R. W. Lintz, Saugus, Ca.
Photo: Nicky Wright*)

OPPOSITE ABOVE: This is the
1966 Cord 8/10 Sportsman
(*Mrs W. P. Conrad, Auburn-
Cord-Duesenberg Museum.
Photo: Nicky Wright*)

OPPOSITE BELOW: The one-
off 1966 Chrysler-engined
Duesenberg built in Italy by
Ghia (*Sam Schwartz,
Auburn-Cord-Duesenberg
Museum. Photo: Nicky
Wright*)

1952 Packard called in 'hotshot appliance salesman' Jim Nance (who had
made marketing history by bringing Hotpoint up to third place in the
household appliance field) in an effort to turn the company around.

Nance, in his four years as President of Packard, 'retired' many of the
older management, ordered the destruction of all Packard's historic files
and parts for obsolete models, had a ghastly new model with electric push-
button-controlled transmission, torsion-bar suspension and all-new bodies
and engines rushed into production with insufficient development, and
merged with that albatross of the classics, Studebaker, which was in such
deep financial trouble that it pulled Packard down. Sales of the 1955
'First Series' developed at Nance's behest were initially good – almost
70,000 were sold – but teething troubles with engine, push-button transmission and load-levelling mechanism brought hostile public reaction in

their wake. Packard, which had embarked on a huge and over-ambitious expansion programme under Nance, sold only 13,193 cars in 1956, ran out of money and, handed over to Studebaker management when Nance left, the group was rapidly swallowed by the Curtiss-Wright Corporation which only wanted it as a tax loss and sold off all the Detroit manufacturing facilities and the Packard proving ground, keeping the Utica engine plant for its own use. All production was moved to Studebaker's South Bend, Indiana, plant, ending Packard plans to produce a new twelve-cylinder luxury car with the traditional radiator. In 1957–58, Studebaker turned out 7431 'Packards' which were Studebakers with grafted-on Packard tail-lights and trim, including 588 of the repulsive Hawk, before dropping the name altogether.

In 1979, however, the Bayliff Coach Corporation of Lima, Ohio, announced that it was beginning production of a revived 'Packard', with the traditional grille and cormorant mascot, based on new Cadillac De Ville chassis, drivetrain and components. This was one of the latest facets of a surprising revival of the classic car concept in America, started in 1964 by the announcement of the 8/10 Cord, an eight-tenth scale replica of the Cord 810, built by Glenn Pray of Tulsa, Oklahoma, using a flat-six Chevrolet Corvair engine to drive the front wheels and with plastics bodywork. The first of these replica Cords was presented to Gordon Buehrig but this bold venture had a chequered career. It was under its third ownership in 1968 when the decision was made to change to a Ford engine, rear-wheel drive, fixed headlamps and glass fibre coachwork. The replica Cord survived until 1973, though production was spasmodic. Appropriately enough, the other components of the Auburn-Cord-Duesenberg

triumvirate have also seen latter-day revivals. An attempt in 1947 to bring back Duesenberg in the guise of a straight-eight designed by August Duesenberg with fuel injection and custom coachwork foundered when it was realized that the $25,000 price tag was more than the postwar market would bear. A similar fate awaited a 1966 attempt to produce a 'modern' Duesenberg, a Ghia-styled behemoth 24 feet in length and costing $25,000; only a prototype of this Virgil Exner-designed four-door sedan was produced.

Then, in 1971, a company in Gardena, California, launched a replica 'SSJ' Duesenberg with a 500bhp supercharged Chrysler engine mounted in a modified Dodge truck chassis and fitted with aluminium bodywork that faithfully reproduced the original. Production was slow, with a $50,000 price tag, and only an estimated twenty-five cars were built by 1977.

As for Auburn, the first replica of the Auburn Speedster came from Glenn Pray in 1966 with a 7 litre Ford V8 while, in 1974, Elegant Motors of Indianapolis brought out *their* version of the Auburn, based on Chevrolet Corvette chassis and running gear. By 1979 they offered a three-car range: 856 Speedster, 898 2 × 2 Phaeton and 898 Phaeton Elegante. There was a third company in the field as well, the Custom Coach Company of Pasadena, whose 876 Speedster and Phaeton, originally offered as assembly kits, were being produced as complete cars in 1979.

Modern 'classics' have appeared, too, which seek to reproduce classic styling features but have modern engines and transmissions and do not seek to be a replica of any bygone marque. Starting with the Excalibur SS in 1964, such vehicles have multiplied in recent years, most notably since the 1973 Arab-Israeli War which saw the start of a growing period of

ABOVE: The Pontiac-based Stutz Blackhawk, launched in 1970, is a Virgil Exner-styled $75,000 luxury car with gold-plated trim (*Mr Irmscher, Fort Wayne, Ind. Photo: Nicky Wright*)

185

ABOVE RIGHT: A 'Modern Classic', the 1979 limited-edition Clenet uses a modified Lincoln chassis beneath its 1930s styling (*Photo : Nicky Wright*)

BELOW RIGHT: The dashboard of the 1979 Clenet (*Photo : Nicky Wright*)

rising prices and falling supplies of petrol. Nowadays the wealthy motorist who wants one of these 'classics' can choose – among others – from Clenet, Diamante and Sceptre cars, all built in limited editions at unlimited prices. Apart from the price tag, can such cars be compared with the great American classics of the 1930s and 1940s? True, they are enjoying great popularity at a time of financial crisis in America, but apart from that there is little similarity. They have been built to respond to a different set of criteria from those which shaped the great classics. These modern limited editions represent a costly passport to freedom from the ever-increasing burden of legislation that is choking the American car industry by compelling it to spend billions of dollars on loading cars with so much safety and emission control equipment that they forfeit a considerable part of their performance. Without the mass producers, however, the modern classicars would waste away, deprived of the Detroit engines and chassis that make them a worthwhile product.

Such modern machinery can never hope to receive accolades like those heaped on the greatest of all the American classics, the Duesenberg: 'Just as its speed exceeds by many miles an hour that of any other automobile, so does it excel in all its other features, including fineness of material, strength, comfort, durability . . . an outstanding automobile from any angle.'

Index